Endorsements

"It's not often a book can be full of valuable information, a wealth of practical application and still be brimming over with inspiration—but *The Lies that Bind* does all three masterfully! Chris Quiring lives what he writes. The Biblical principles here are written in his heart. He carries a deep, God given authority to instruct and challenge others with a depth of experience, knowledge and wisdom. Every Christian needs to read this book and then read it again!"

—BILL PAYNE, International Speaker & Founder
of Truth Box Ministries

"Chris is a gifted leader, and in addition to being a brilliant guy, he has a huge heart. This book will open the reader's eyes and awaken their hearts to the lies that have kept them from the abundant life Jesus came to bring. I highly recommend you sit with this book and allow God to do a great work in your life."

—GREG ATKINSON, Author, Speaker, & Founder
of the First Impressions Conference

"Filled with interesting stories, solidly Biblical principles, and practical application to the reality of life in our day, *The Lies That Bind* is a must read for all who long to experience the spiritual freedom that Jesus has provided. Chris' pastor's heart and his deep desire to have the people of God experience all that Jesus promises is written on every page. I loved this book!"

—BOB BEASLEY, Chief Ministry Officer,
Bible League of Canada

"With Biblical knowledge and insightful observations from his life, Chris Quiring points the way toward experiencing true freedom. Chris' transparent honesty invokes the same in his reader. I found myself noticing the lies that have crept into my own life and the harm they've caused. With well-placed quotes, skilled retellings of stories from the Bible, and a dash of humor, Chris outlines practical strategies to aid the reader in their spiritual formation. His pastoral heart shines on every page."

—LAURA FOX, Author of
The Missing Moved in: A Grief Journey

With keen insight and storied examples, Chris Quiring has written an invaluable work of how to live fearlessly in a world of lies. This book will be a counsel of hope and joy for the many who read it—and the encouragement we need, especially today in this time of cascading crises of false hopes and empty promises. The book begins with a premise that plays out throughout the following chapters that when it comes to lies, we must name them to tame them. And Chris poignantly does that.

—ANTHONY J. DOES, Pastor, Author, Dreamer

Chris has a powerful yet practical way of communicating the gospel. His heart to see people living an abundant life, clothed in truth, is strongly conveyed on every page. *The Lies That Bind* will help you find freedom through Jesus and bring you closer to the heart of the Father.

—BROOKE NICHOLLS, Juno Nominated Worship Leader &
Recording Artist

"Pastor Chris Quiring hits the nail on the head with his treatment of the devil's many deceptions that plague the follower of Jesus. This book is a rubber-meets-the-road manual for the serious believer who wants to live the victorious Christian life. Pastor Quiring's engaging style and down to earth stories from his own experiences give you the feeling that he is a player-coach—he gives you the truths from Scripture to address the problems but then also gets right in there with you, letting you know that he is fighting the same battle. Make this book an annual read!"

—BRIAN HORROBIN, Pastor of First Baptist Church

"Jesus was clear, He came to give us life and life to the full, but the problem is we buy the lies of the world and live beneath the life Jesus intended us to have. Chris does a masterful job of exposing the lies that bind us, while combining powerful truth that's rooted in scripture with personal real life stories. He has a gracious way of exposing these lies while also drawing you to the life that Jesus intended."

—RON BAKER, Pastor of VitalPoint Church

"With godly wisdom, testimonial warmth, and a tasteful touch of humor, *The Lies That Bind* will equip you and those you're discipling to discern and demolish the strongholds stopping us from engaging in more faithful gospel mission together. I challenge fellow Christ-followers of all ages to supplement our regular Bible study with this practical playbook!"

—CORY MCKENNA, The Equipping Evangelist & Founder of The Cross Current

EXPOSING THE LIES KEEPING YOU FROM A
RICH & MEANINGFUL LIFE // CHRIS QUIRING

Contents

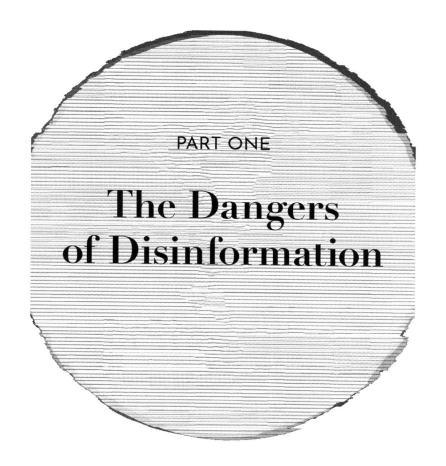

PART ONE

The Dangers of Disinformation

1

The Rhythms
of Victory

There's an old parable told of a man who was convinced he was too light. For some reason he was sure that if he walked outside, just as he was, he would float off into the clouds and never be seen again. This thought terrified him. It robbed him of his sleep. It occupied his waking hours and invaded whatever quiet he could find. No one knew why he felt this way, but it was impossible to convince him otherwise. Somehow this deep-seated fear had become a living, breathing part of him.

As the fear grew, it became harder and harder to hide. Every time he left the house he would line his pockets with weights—trinkets and scrap metal, nuts and bolts, and whatever heavy object he could find—all in the hopes it would keep him tethered to the ground.

As you could imagine, it was quite a sight. The load was so heavy, his body strained under the weight. His neighbors could easily identify his sunken silhouette from a mile away. In the past, he'd often watched the sun rise as he walked, or watched birds in the sky; now the only thing he could see as he ambled down the road was the miles of concrete beneath his feet.

That was how he lived his life—carrying the weight of the world on his shoulders.

A story is a remarkable thing. There's a reason Jesus chose to speak primarily in riddles and parables. A story forces you to not just think about truth, but feel it. Stories connect with us on a level that no other form of communication can reach. I know this tale of the man afraid of floating away is fictional, and it exists only in our imagination. But the strangest thing is, each time I read it, I feel something. This deep sense of empathy.

Logically I know it doesn't make sense. Was the man too light? Was he so dangerously thin that the laws of physics no longer applied? Would he have floated off into the sky if he didn't weigh himself down? Not in a thousand years. He was no more at risk of accidental liftoff than I am of spontaneous human combustion. Yet this story affects me. Why?

Because I've been there before—and so have you. We know what this feels like. I've seen it in my own life and the lives of countless people I've known. It's a story of what happens when we live in a world that no longer corresponds to reality. It's a story of what happens when we begin to live out the lies we've been told and to carry around the baggage they bring. We don't realize that they're lies; to us they're as true as anything else we believe—and that's precisely what makes them so dangerous.

The longer I've followed Jesus, the more I've come to believe that a lie is a powerful thing that can change the course of your life.

You can trace most of the problems you face each day to a lie like this. Whether it was the fight you just had with your spouse, or that nagging fear that stalks you at night, or the anxious thoughts that circle in your head as you try to fall asleep— underneath each of them is a lie you've believed. Beneath every struggle with negative thoughts, every fight with temptation, or every battle with low self-esteem—there's inevitably a lie. A misperception. A twisting of the truth.

You've been fed a falsehood that seemed reasonable at the time, and it has shaped who you are inside. These are what I've called the lies that bind.

The Rhythms of Victory

We all have them. Each and every one of us. We've accumulated them along the way as accidental souvenirs of our travels. The problem is that we aren't aware of them, and until we identify them, they'll continue to wreak havoc on our hearts and lives.

Our goal in the pages ahead is to unmask these untruths and break the hold they have on our story. They've hijacked our thoughts and sabotaged our relationships for far too long. They've been at the center of our worst choices, and led us down the paths we wish we'd never taken.

Once you see the lies for what they are, your story will instantly begin to make more sense. (I know mine has.) Once you recognize them, you'll understand why you took wrong paths, and the emotions that drove you there. More importantly, once you see them you'll be able to choose a different path when you face them again. No longer will they dictate your decisions, alter your perceptions, or drag you back whenever you start making progress.

Jesus promised us that by holding to his teaching, we'll know the truth, and the truth will set us free (John 8:32). It's one of the most amazing and revealing promises Jesus makes to us in the Gospels—because if truth is what frees us, then lies must be what holds us in chains.

Through a process I call recognition training, we'll learn to discern the lies that are camouflaged in our hearts, and how to unwind their influence in our lives. Though not always sequential, this process involves three steps that we'll interact deeply with, as we examine the most salient and effective lies in our world today. Here are those steps:

1. Identify.
2. Trace.
3. Replace.

This is the rhythm I want to teach you to make a part of your life.

5

To break the power these lies hold over us, we must first identify them. *We must name them to tame them.* In the chapters that comprise the heart of this book, we'll unpack the most common falsehoods that have evaded our defenses and made a home in our souls, because that's where their spiritual energy resides. Once you're more aware of what these lies look like, you'll be able to recognize them in whatever disguise they arrive in, and call them out.

Next we'll trace them back to their source. These lies did not spontaneously generate or appear out of thin air; they originated from somewhere—or rather, from some*one*. Once you realize who's lying to you, and that he's literally hellbent on your destruction, you'll find him infinitely easier to resist.

Finally, we'll replace those lies with truth. None of the previous steps will mean anything if this isn't our ultimate destination. The antidote to the poison of a lie is truth, and truth is the key to our chains. The living, breathing words of God are the most effective weapon in our arsenal against the subterfuge of the enemy, and we must use God's words as Jesus did to break the power of deceit.

Jesus died to bring us freedom. He promised us abundant life. He bled to purchase our victory. These three things are our birthright as children of God, and it's high time we claimed them! After all, we are sons and daughters of the King.

There are times when such a life feels like only a mirage on the horizon, forever just beyond our reach—like a song you can hear in another room, but you can't quite make out the melody. But know this: One of the most astonishing truths of the gospel is that freedom and abundance are exactly what Jesus is offering you and me.

Our daily struggles are rooted in the lies that bind, and the workings of the enemy. This book is dedicated to unmasking those two things.

2

Unmasking
the Liar

God doesn't always speak the way you expect him to. And neither does he speak where you assume. Sometimes it's in the least likely spaces that he reveals something to you. This was one of those times.

It was the last round of the afternoon. Some friends and I had met at a huge outdoor paintball field tucked in between two of the Great Lakes. It was an afternoon of exhaustion and adrenaline. If you've never tried paintball, you must. It's entirely worth the welts.

Not long before we called it quits, I decided to try my luck alone and headed into the woods looking for a place to hide. No partners, no friends. Just me.

After a little searching, I found the perfect spot. It was a tree, or a group of trees rather, growing together from the same roots. From the outside it simply looked like one seamless trunk, but if you looked hard enough, your patience and persistence were rewarded. There was a small gap out of sight that opened to a cavity—just large enough for me to fit inside.

I climbed in and waited for someone to walk by. A few minutes later, through slivered threads of light sneaking between the trunks, I saw him. A friend under any other circumstance. He was alone, cautiously walking with his gun raised, completely unaware he'd been seen.

I could barely contain my excitement. My heart was nearly beating out of my chest. I kept watching, frozen in time, as he took step after step closer to my location—oblivious to the danger he was in. Every muscle and tendon in my body was drawn like a bowstring. When he finally ventured near enough and turned away—I jumped out of my blind and lit him up like a Christmas tree!

Seriously.

I rode that double trigger like it was a full-blown automatic rifle, and emptied half my store of ammunition into his camouflage vest. It was quite a sight. When I was finished he was so covered in paint, he could have easily auditioned for the Blue Man Group.

Only later did I find out that when you have a clean shot at someone, it's proper etiquette to fire only once and allow your enemy to bow out in peace. But I was inexperienced and overzealous in equal measure—and my friend paid the price that day.

And boy, he was *mad*.

I think you could hear the streak of four letter words that flowed out of him from every acre in that field! He demanded to know who I was, over and over—but I kept my rifle up and my mask on. I wasn't going to tell him. To this day he still doesn't know it was me.

I've thought back on that experience many times since, and I realized God had shown me something in that moment. (God often speaks in the most unlikely situations.) I realized he taught me something I was going to need in years to come, and it was as simple as it was powerful:

The most dangerous enemy is always the one you cannot see.

When you know who you're up against and where to find them, you can plan ahead and watch for signs of danger. You can recognize when they're on the move and the traps laid out in front of you. But the most dangerous enemy is always the one you can't see.

I'm sure my friend would agree.

As we begin to unpack the lies that have made a home inside your life and are wreaking havoc on your heart, this story is a good place to begin. Not just as a long-overdue apology to a friend, but as a picture of what's happening inside us. What makes these lies so effective is the fact that they're invisible to the one who's caught in them. Lies don't always come dressed in red, carrying a pitchfork; instead they masquerade as truth. In fact, some of the most dangerous lies we believe are not outright lies, but half truths. They have just enough substance to confuse us. As Charles Spurgeon once said, "Discernment is not a matter of simply telling the difference between right and wrong; rather it is telling the difference between right and almost right."[1]

If you've ever confronted a friend or a family member, you know how true this can be. Not every intervention results in an awakening. We're always the last ones to see the things in our lives that need to change, and it's nearly impossible for someone else to expose our blind spots. After all, that's why they're called blind spots. If we knew they were lies, we would discard them without a second thought. But as long as they stay hidden, we struggle under their weight.

There's another layer to this story, one that we don't talk about enough these days, even within the church. It's the battle being fought behind the scenes. Our battle is not just with the lies our culture has told us and the wrong ways we've come to understand the world around us. Our ultimate fight is with the liar that spoke them in the first place.

Each and every lie that exists ultimately traces back to the one whom Jesus called the "father of lies." If you follow the lies back long enough, their winding path will inevitably lead back to him. You may have heard it from a parent or a friend, who heard it from their parents or their friends, but that lie ultimately began in the mouth of the enemy of our souls. Lies are his ammunition, and he is the enemy in the trees.

It has been said that the devil's single greatest trick has been to convince the world he doesn't exist. But Jesus knew otherwise. There *is* a devil, and he's literally hellbent on our destruction. His mission is to steal, kill, and destroy, as Jesus tells us in John 10:10. In Scripture he's called the Satan, the evil one, the tempter, the destroyer, the deceiver, the accuser, and the great dragon who deceives the world. Each title is describing the same being—the enemy of our souls. John Mark Comer observes that each of these "is a title, not a name. Some biblical scholars argue this is a subtle dig from Jesus, a deliberate snub; his rival doesn't even get a name. Others read it as a sign of how dangerous he finds [him]."[2] Either way, Jesus is talking about some*one*, not just some*thing*, and we do well to heed his warning.

The truth is, we're in a battle, a cosmic battle for our hearts and minds. We have an enemy who's alive, present, and active in our life. He'll do whatever he can to thwart the sovereign destiny God has chosen and laid out in front of us. And here's the crucial thing: Each time, he'll use lies to do it.

It turns out that the world we live in isn't composed only of what we can see. Reality is far more than skin deep. There's a reality behind our reality—a spiritual world just as real as the ground beneath your feet. If we're going to win this war, we need to dig below the surface and get to the heart of our struggle.

Perhaps you've been asking yourself questions like these:

Why do I give in to the same temptations time and time again, even though they were empty last time?

Why can't I let go of the past and the wrongs that have been done to me?

Why don't my relationships last?

Who do I always feel so down?

Unmasking the Liar

Why do I struggle with negative thoughts and low self-esteem?

Why can't I let go of my fears? Why do they still push me around?

This is why: *We have an enemy who has been lying to us from the beginning.*

Whether it's temptation, discouragement, accusation, or the tormenting power of a grudge—each stream traces back to the same headwaters. They're the lies the enemy uses to keep us from the abundant life Jesus has promised us. They're the chains he convinces us to submit to. These are the lies that bind, and this book is an exercise in unmasking them.

The enemy of our souls thrives in the shadows, and it's time we turned on the light.

3

The Life Cycle
of a Lie

As you begin to uncover these untruths that have been buried and camouflaged in your hearts for some time, you'll notice another characteristic about them. They're remarkably stubborn. They've become rather attached to their surroundings, and have made quite a home for themselves in our emotions and memories.

Lies that have lived inside us for years aren't just enmeshed; they're entrenched. Identifying them is where we must begin, but eviction is no easy feat.

I've known many friends who've been adopted by a loving, caring family who raised them like their very own flesh and blood, yet deep down they still struggle with the lie that they're unwanted. I think every adopted child wrestles with this. It's hard for any human being to come to terms with the fact that those who should have loved them more than anyone on earth chose instead to give them away. This lie manifests itself in all sorts of different areas, and in seemingly unrelated things. And though the adopted persons intellectually know the truth—that they're not just loved but have been *chosen* by their adoptive parents—they still struggle with the deception they grew up believing: that they're unlovable. It's the lie the enemy whispers in their ear every opportunity he gets, and the emotion is tremendously hard to shake. All the counseling in the world won't result in lasting change until this lie is called out and replaced.

The Life Cycle of a Lie

LIES BECOME STRONGHOLDS

Paul talks about our war with such lies in his second letter to the church in Corinth. Listen to what he says:

> For though we live in the world, we do not wage war as the world does. The weapons we fight with are not the weapons of the world. On the contrary, they have divine power to demolish strongholds. We demolish arguments and every pretension that sets itself up against the knowledge of God, and we take captive every thought to make it obedient to Christ. (2 Corinthians 10:4-5)

When Paul is looking for a word to describe what happens when a lie roots down and makes a home for itself in our lives, he uses the word "stronghold." It's a remarkable word. In this context, Paul is talking primarily about the big lies woven into the fabric of our culture. These are the lies that are so prevalent that no one even bothers to question them.

The word for "stronghold" in Greek is *ochuroma,* from a verb that literally means "to fortify." It was a word they used in the ancient Near East to describe fortresses that were usually constructed on the highest hill, with walls as much as twenty feet thick. When an enemy breached the city gates, the king and the nobles were whisked away and locked in such a stronghold for safekeeping. It was where they armored up and hunkered down.

I visited the ancient fortress of Masada years ago. It's a breathtaking sight. It was a stronghold built by King Herod on a 1,300-foot-high plateau overlooking the Dead Sea. Surrounded by cliffs, and with defenses carved right into the side of the mountain, it was nearly impenetrable. It was so tall and so well built that a small garrison of Israeli soldiers held off the army of the mighty Roman Empire for seven months.

This is the word picture Paul used when he was describing

the lies we've come to believe and what we're up against. A stone fortress. Well stocked, well supplied, and armed to the teeth.

Once we identify these strongholds, our job is not to negotiate with them, but to tear them down brick by brick. Remember, this is war. Our job is to raze them and rebuild in their place. If we let a stronghold stand, it will remain an outpost of the enemy, and he'll use it to continue harassing us for years to come. So down it must come. Think of it as a kind of holy demolition.

Once we've identified the strongholds, the way we tear them down is with truth. That's the weapon we fight with that has "divine power to demolish strongholds." We learn this incredibly powerful process of taking every thought captive to make it obedient to Christ. This battle begins in the mind. We must grab hold of those unhealthy and untrue thoughts, and replace them with the truth.

Identify, trace, and replace. This is the rhythm of victory, and it's exactly how Paul is calling us to fight back.

LIES BECOME RUTS

After a lie has become a stronghold in our lives, it becomes a rut that we consistently fall into, and we often have a hard time escaping. If you've ever struggled with recurring negative thoughts that you just can't seem to break free from, you know exactly what this feels like.

I grew up in Winnipeg, Manitoba, which has the unenviable title of the coldest major city in the world. In the winter, when the snow would fall by the foot and refuse to melt, the cars would inevitably wear ruts into the roads. The packed snow walls would grow up to ten inches deep. After a few weeks, the ruts would ice over and solidify, and even the snow plows were unable to scrape them off. In February, a simple trip to the grocery store is treacherous.

Here's the thing about those ruts: Once you're in one, it's

incredibly hard to get out. I remember riding as a child with my mom as she drove, and she tried to break out of one of these ruts and change lanes—we spun 720 degrees in the middle of a four-lane highway; it was only by the grace of God that we didn't wind up in a massive accident. If you travel even further north from Winnipeg, it only gets worse. There's a sign near the Arctic Circle that says, "Choose your rut carefully, because you'll be in it for the next sixty miles." It's an apt warning.

Our thoughts and our habits function very much the same. We get stuck in these thought ruts that are extremely hard to escape.

One of the curious characteristics of lies is that they're strengthened by repetition. I wish this wasn't true, but the evidence is overwhelming. Research has proven that the most effective way to get someone to believe a lie is to simply repeat it.[3] If you've ever wondered why politicians stick to their talking points and seem incapable of answering straightforward questions, this is it. If they can simply tell you the same lie long enough, there's a good chance you'll start believing it. Sociologists even have a name for this effect: the illusory truth effect. The more we hear a lie, the more likely we are to believe it. Each time you hear it, it gets a little less crazy and a little more ingrained.

Whether that lie is from a president, a news anchor, or an ex-boyfriend, the more we hear something, the more likely we are to believe it. These lies become ruts in our neural pathways and our emotional memory.

One of the lies I grew up believing had to do with money. It started fairly innocently. It was my dad who passed it along to me. I've heard it said that every parent owes their firstborn an apology. After raising three kids, I can't help but agree. (Sorry, Nate!) Our eldest kids are the guinea pig for all our parenting strategies, the good, the bad, and the ugly.

My father wanted to teach me to have a healthy relationship with money, so he constantly reminded me to save as much as I could, and when I spent it to make sure I took care of whatever I bought. You may be thinking, *That's great advice!* And it was, until it sunk in a little too deeply. It was a steady drumbeat from him throughout my childhood. His was the voice I heard constantly in my ear every time I was faced with a decision.

He would say it about anything I ever spent money on. When I bought a bike, he would remind me again and again to lock it up, or some kid would steal it. Every time I left the house, those words would follow me out the door. Then one day when he drove by the convenience store at the end of our street and saw my bike unlocked, he stole it.

Yes, you read that right. My father stole my bike.

He was so tired of reminding me he decided to make me feel it—and boy, did it work! I ran home crying so hard I could barely breathe, realizing he'd been right all along—only to find my bike in the back of his pickup truck as I walked up the driveway. Needless to say, that left a mark on my heart.

Unfortunately, as I grew up I had trouble letting anyone use my things. I couldn't let them go, for fear that they would get broken. I kept hearing my father's voice ringing in my ears. And as I got older, my wallet would creak whenever I opened it. In the first few years of our marriage, I would micromanage every red cent, and I'm sure it drove my wife to distraction. Inadvertently, I began to believe it was up to me, not God, to provide for my family—and that's where the deception began. Watching my father go bankrupt a few years later only reinforced this stronghold in me.

The thing is, it's a lie. I am *not* the one who provides. The truth is that God is my provider. He is the one who watches over me. Yes, we're to be wise with what he's given us, but we're just middle managers; God is the source.

Sometimes lies aren't just complete falsehoods, but truth

that's veered out of balance. In fact, that's one of the best definitions of heresy. It's the half truths that are always the hardest to see. The truth about money and possessions is that we are blessed to be a blessing, and when God gives us good things, he calls us to share it with those around us. There is freedom, life, and security in this truth—and it needed to replace the lie that was in my heart.

Now each time that lie creeps back into my head, I grab hold of it, take it captive, and make it obedient to Christ.

Identify, trace, and *replace.* We must flatten those ruts that have worn their way into our souls, or we'll spend the rest of our lives reliving them.

But there's one final stage in the life cycle of a lie.

LIES BECOME LENSES

There's more at stake than simply the little corner of our hearts where these lies dwell. Sure, they'll affect that part of your story and the people who live there with you, but they'll also become a lens through which you see the world. They'll discolor everything else you see.

Lies inevitably become lenses. Once you allow them into your perception, they'll distort your vision. This is why we overreact in some circumstances and underreact in others. A situation that's really only a two out of ten in importance becomes a nine out of ten in our thinking, and we blow up accordingly. When your husband says he's too tired to talk tonight, what you hear is, "Our relationship is falling apart." That wasn't what he said or meant, but it's exactly what we heard. The world of psychology calls this overregulation. I teach this concept to almost every one of the people I counsel. The reason we overreact is that we don't see the situation clearly; we're staring at it through a faulty set of lenses.

I wear red tinted glasses at work—not because I'm an international rock star, or any kind of fashion trend setter, but because screens give me headaches. I know, way less cool. I tend to get a rare form of migraines from most computer and TV screens, so I wear these special tinted lenses—which, to be more accurate, are actually rose colored.

So yes, I see life through rose colored glasses.

It's really helpful for work, but terrible when I'm trying to buy clothes online. I always have to bring my wife in to make sure I'm not buying a hot pink sweater, thinking it's maroon or crimson. These lenses of mine color everything I look at, and I don't see things the way they are.

In psychology circles, this is sometimes called cognitive bias, which is "a systematic error in thinking that occurs when people are processing and interpreting information in the world around them," and this "affects the decisions and judgments they make."[4] Translation: A distorted version of reality leads to mismatched emotions and poor decisions.

This is what lies do to our vision. They become a lens through which you see the world. When you believe all men are untrustworthy, you'll start every relationship with those glasses on. If you believe God will one day abandon you, you'll see that possibility in every tough situation you face.

In the first few years of marriage, my wife never accepted my apologies. I could never understand why. It was a puzzle I couldn't solve until I learned more about her story. People in her life had used the words "I'm sorry" again and again without ever really meaning them. Inside she'd been convinced that those two words are never sincere and mean virtually nothing. That isn't true, but I can completely understand why she felt that way. They were glasses she was given, and through which she saw each of our conversations.

If we want to see clearly, we must remove the lies that are coloring everything we see. How do we do that? We must learn to recognize those lies. We must train ourselves to spot the deception through a little process I've called recognition training, to help us learn the art of lie detection.

RECOGNITION TRAINING

A few summers ago, my son challenged me to a game of chess. We were camping that week, and you can fill only so much of the day with suntanning and eating s'mores, so I accepted. Actually, I was thrilled he asked. He was in third grade, and to be honest with you, I thought it would be a walk in the park.

The first two matches finished much how I would have hoped. I won, but Nate took enough pieces to feel like he'd put up a fight. But the third game didn't play out so smoothly. Halfway through I suddenly realized I was painfully down in material and was about to lose, if I didn't do something quickly.

This possibility had never occurred to me. I started to panic. I could feel my stomach begin to turn, and I was short of breath. A tremor worked its way into my hand, and I frantically scanned the board looking for a way out. Every father knows his days as king of the hill are numbered, but I thought I would wear that crown a little longer than his eighth birthday. Then, at the very last moment, I found it.

Thank you, Lord. I just barely managed to escape.

My son doesn't know this, but after that near loss, I hid in the trailer and desperately searched the internet for how to play chess. He probably thought I was taking a nap, but I was scouring the web for help. He didn't realize that for the rest of the week, he was playing against not just me, but the accumulated wisdom of cyberspace. I'm not proud of it, but I needed something! Anything to help me stay in the game. I wasn't ready to lose to him yet.

Interestingly enough, one of the main ways to improve your chess game is to complete puzzles. Over and over they'll show you a potential situation, a snapshot in a hypothetical game against a hypothetical opponent, and you have to work your way out of it. Avid players complete hundreds of these puzzles a day.

The idea is rather simple: The more puzzles you complete, the more traps you'll recognize. When you're in a situation like that again in the future, your mind will spark and your synapses will fire, and you'll remember. You'll recognize the pattern, and the alarm will sound. You've seen this before, and you know how to escape!

Lies function in the same way. They follow a recognizable pattern. And the more we make ourselves aware of those patterns, the better prepared we'll be. Once we're able to identify those deceptions the moment they arrive, then trace them back to their source, we'll begin to shed the layers we've been carrying for so long.

Much of this book is built on that principle. It's the fundamental idea at the heart of it. In many ways, we're about to embark on a type of recognition training. As we stare intently at the lies woven into the fabric of our lives, we'll learn how to recognize and defeat them.

In my own battle with these very lies and strategies of the enemy, I've come to believe that awareness is everything. Some lies have taken me years to recognize and resist, because of how deeply they were buried in my story. But naming them has instantly stolen much of their power.

Our freedom and victory hinge on our ability to identify these lies in real time, and reject them. That's the path Jesus is laying out for us—to know the truth, and have the truth set us free.

I believe with all my heart that through this process of learning what these deceptions are, we'll be able to identify them the moment they arrive, trace them back to their source, and replace them with truth. We can finally empty the scrap metal from our pockets, take off our trench coats, and begin to walk in the freedom Jesus bought for you and me.

PART TWO

The Lies

4

The Lie of: Division

If You Don't Agree with Me, You're My Enemy

There is neither Jew nor Gentile,
neither slave nor free, nor is there male and female,
for you are all one in Christ Jesus.
GALATIANS 3:28

My younger brother is a therapist, and several years ago he was working for a private counseling clinic. He had a good rapport with the staff and a good relationship with the managing partner, and he really enjoyed the work. After a year or so, he was asked if he would like to stay on a more permanent basis. If he was interested, there was a contract on his desk waiting for a signature. They gave him a few days to think about it. In the end, he decided he would like to continue in this position.

He wrote an email to the owner of the firm to communicate his decision to re-sign the contract. The next day, when he arrived at work, it was like a cold front had moved in. His boss barely gave him the time of day and wouldn't speak to him. She walked by without the slightest acknowledgment, and gave him the cold shoulder every time she passed. (By the way, I find it hilarious how many dysfunctional interactions happen at counseling firms full of MA's and PhD's in psychology.)

After a few days of this, my brother confronted his boss: "What's going on? Where's all this tension coming from?"

She replied, "Well, you quit. How did you think it was going to be?"

Utterly confused, he said, "What do you mean, I quit? I sent you an email to renew my contract."

"No you didn't," she replied. "You quit. You decided *not* to renew your contract."

Nothing made sense. Totally confused, he went back and reread his email, and sure enough, she was right. He'd quit. He didn't mean to, but he did. All he forgot was one simple little punctuation, and it was enough to nearly cost him his job. All he forgot was a hyphen.

What is "re-sign" without the hyphen?

Resign!

In the email to her, he'd written that he'd thought long about it, and he wanted to "resign my contract."

I would like to say that they all had a good laugh about it afterward, but the damage was done. If only life were that simple. He managed to keep his job, though just barely, but the relationship was never the same. So remember, when your grammar teacher tells you that something's important—she isn't kidding!

This story is both one of the funniest and most frustrating stories I know. Somehow a simple little miscommunication resulted in a series of incredibly strained relationships, and it nearly changed the trajectory of my brother's professional life. A wise man once observed that the single biggest problem in communication is the illusion that it has taken place.[5] Seventeen years into ministry, I wholeheartedly agree.

DIVIDE AND CONQUER

What troubles me about my brother's story is how strangely familiar it seems. I've never had a hyphen cost me a relationship or a job, but I've seen versions of it all my life. How many times have we tried to say one thing, but the person across the table hears precisely the opposite? How many times have our words passed through a wormhole in the ten feet between us and come out entirely different on the other side? How many times has a dialogue turned into two dueling monologues, where no one's listening and both parties just want to keep speaking?

Communication is hard, all on its own. I've been married for seventeen years, and even though I speak publicly for a living, my wife could tell you a mountain of stories that would suggest otherwise. In fact, I was so bad at asking her out the day we started dating, she didn't even realize what had happened. It was a communication train wreck. I walked away from that talk excited that we'd started dating; she walked away thinking, "Boy, he seems nice!" For months we actually celebrated different anniversaries!

But there's more going on here than just our inability. The truth is, there are gremlins in the machine. There's actually a third actor in so many of these dramas that we never seem to see, one who has twisted our words and misrepresented our intentions more times than we can count.

What we learn about our enemy in Scripture is that he's intent on dividing us every chance he gets. He works tirelessly to separate us from the core relationships and people in our lives. Instead of fighting us all together, it's far easier for him to challenge us one at a time. To peel us away from the pack, he'll do whatever he can whenever he can.

It happens in a hundred different ways. Sometimes he'll make sure you overhear the worst seven words of a conversation that make it sound like people are talking about you. I've literally watched this happen in the hallway of our church, and I felt like chasing the angry person and saying, "No! You don't understand! That's not what they meant!" Have you ever caught just enough of two people talking to make you upset, but nowhere near enough to know what they were actually saying? At other times our enemy will convince you there's an ulterior motive behind that email someone sent or that conversation you had. Having seen this play out far too many times, I've come to believe that these aren't accidents, but orchestrations. They're simply timed too perfectly.

Misunderstanding and misinformation are dangerous tools in the hands of the enemy, but there's a lie we've come to believe that has proven far more deadly. The king of all the relational lies which the enemy whispers in our ear is this one:

If you don't agree with me, you're my enemy.

Take a moment and think of how prevalent that lie is in our world right now. I can pretty much guarantee you've seen it today. Go take a stroll on your favorite social media platform, and look for it—it's literally everywhere. It's dripping from the trench warfare of the comments section, and it's the driving force behind the algorithm populating your feed. Watch the news for an hour and listen for it—you'll hear it echo over and over in the way they talk about "us" and "them," whether explicitly or implicitly. In fact, I would go so far as to say that our world right now is being torn apart almost single-handedly by this entrenched lie: If someone doesn't agree with me, they're my enemy.

Whether it's a disagreement over which politician you support, which team you root for, or where you land on the contentious issues of our day, we've become a society where what you think determines who you can associate with. We've drawn line after line in the sand and formed into tribes on each side. Tribalism is tearing apart our churches, families, and countries, and no one seems to be able to stem the bleeding.

I worry sometimes that we're witnessing the slow and painful death of the art of conversation. Long gone is the free exchange of ideas where two people can share differing perspectives and simply agree to disagree.

I pastor a church in Canada, and when conflict arises, I can tell you that trying to keep both sides together feels like standing with one foot on the dock and the other in a shaky canoe. It's uncomfortable to say the least. Sometimes no matter what you try, you can still feel each side slip further and further apart with each passing day.

My experience isn't unique. It doesn't matter what the issue is, all conflict feels this way. In fact, you may be bridging those very same gaps with your friends and family.

This lie will worm its way into your relationships and into your workplace. It will show up in your marriage and in your family. The enemy will slip it into your conversations around the dinner table at Thanksgiving, and into every interaction with your teenage kids as they leave for school. In each and every crack, he'll pour like water and expand like ice. Anywhere and everywhere he can, he'll sow seeds of division in your life and in your community.

A BROKEN FAMILY TREE

Sadly, this is nowhere more evident than in church history. These lies run deep in your ancestral story and mine, but there's no family the enemy is trying to tear apart more than the family of God. With enough time and enough paper, you could sketch out the last two thousand years of the church's family tree, but the endless story of broken branches and severed limbs just might be too painful to see.

Jesus made a spectacular promise to us in Matthew 16:18. He promised that he himself will build his church, and that the gates of hell will not prevail against it.

Think on that for a moment. It's an amazing picture.

The church of Jesus Christ is an unstoppable force when we allow the Lord to work within it. It's so strong that not even the gates of hell will be able to withstand its assault. Jesus is telling us there's power—chain-breaking, mountain-taking, claim-staking power—when the church moves as one!

If this is true—why hasn't history read like this prophecy? Why do we have such a broken and divisive legacy?

The answer lies in this lie we've believed—that if anyone disagrees with me, they're my enemy. Instead of fighting against the church, our enemy would far rather convince us to fight against each other.

Brilliant, isn't it? Why fight a war when you can simply divide your foe and let your enemy fight against himself?

DISCORD, DISSENSION, AND FACTIONS

In Galatians 5, Paul lays out how sin works its way into our lives. It's a laundry list of broken paths and dead ends—and look at how many of them are related to unity:

> The acts of the flesh are obvious: sexual immorality, impurity and debauchery; idolatry and witchcraft; *hatred, discord, jealousy,* fits of rage, *selfish ambition, dissensions, factions* and *envy*; drunkenness, orgies, and the like. I warn you, as I did before, that those who live like this will not inherit the kingdom of God. (Galatians 5:19-21)

Of the fifteen different acts of the flesh Paul mentions here, at least seven have to do with relationships, and three of them are just different words for division: *discord, dissension*, and *factions*. Instead of mentioning division once, he does it three different times with three different words that essentially mean the same thing.

If you read Paul's letters, you know how often division rears its ugly head. It was a cancerous problem in the early church, cutting short the lives of countless relationships and communities.

I could trace this through the entire biblical timeline for you, but I'm willing to bet you've already seen this lie at work in your own city—split churches, broken Bible study groups, and families or friendships left in shambles after the steamroller of division rolled through.

I've personally watched a church come apart at the seams, and it was one of the saddest storylines of my life. The word *split* is far too clean a word to describe the carnage that happens when a body of faith divides. It's the kind of wound that never completely heals, and there are times I still grieve over what could have been. Lifelong friendships and family ties were torn apart in a matter of weeks. After having lived through a split like this, I'm convinced that if you could do an autopsy or some kind of post mortem on the circumstances that led to it, you would find this lie at its heart, and the enemy's fingerprints all over each and every part.

Throughout church history, there has been no shortage of topics to fight over. Human beings are drawn to conflict like a moth to a flame. Issues that divide are almost magnetic. We often call them wedge issues—a quite accurate way to describe them, as we'll soon see. From the very beginning of the church, there have been countless reasons to divide into warring factions and dig in for a fight.

When I was growing up it was "worship wars" that tore churches apart. In other generations it has been dress codes, or liturgy, or Bible translations ("King James Version only!"), or all kinds of doctrinal disputes.

Don't get me wrong; some doctrinal issues are absolutely deal breakers. I'm not saying bad theology doesn't matter. There are fundamental truths we must have in common to remain united. But we desperately need to know how to identify them.

OPEN AND CLOSED HANDS

The best way I've come to understand this is to think of closed-handed issues versus open-handed issues.

Right now, as you read, make a fist. Let that closed hand represent a container for all the central truths of the Christian faith. These are the truths about who Jesus is—the Son of God, born of a virgin, sinless, perfect, the pure sacrifice for our sins, risen from the dead, and reigning at the right hand of God. Along with them are the truths about the character of God—his righteousness, grace, love, and his attributes as creator, savior, and king. These are the deepest and clearest truths of the gospel, and they go in a closed hand.

On these things we will not budge. They are not up for debate.

Now with your other hand, open it palm up. This is where the open-handed issues go—issues like worship music style, dress code, church governance, and so many of the hot button topics in the church. Issues like whether Harry Potter is dangerous, and whether yoga is a tool of the enemy. At the end of the day, these are issues on which committed Christians who love Jesus have simply come to different conclusions. They may make a lot of noise in discussions around the table, but the topics are not fundamental. We can agree to disagree and still remain united. In these areas, we're to hold our convictions loosely, because there are some things God hasn't been as clear on as others.

What we must realize is that the church is full of both of these kinds of issues. The problem is, the majority of the issues that have divided the church have belonged in the open hand, but the enemy has squeezed them between us and driven us apart.

You can distill this ethos down to a famous phrase that goes back a number of centuries: "In the essentials, unity; in non-essentials, liberty; in all things, charity."[6] Those words should be written on the front door of every church in America, and visible every time we go out into the world. In the fundamental, rock-solid, essential truths of Scripture—we find our unity. *Closed hand.* There can be nothing less. This is the foundation of our fellowship. In other areas, where faithful Christians who love Jesus disagree—there must be freedom. *Open hand.* Here we must create space for each of us to follow our conscience and the Spirit's leading. Meanwhile, in everything there must be charity, love, and respect.

Let me ask you a few questions. What if a person's political or cultural leanings didn't have to cost you their friendship? Wouldn't that be wonderful? What if it was possible to actually disagree with someone else and still get along? What if another person's music preference didn't exclude them from your life? I know it's a grand vision, but wouldn't you want to live in a world like that? I know I do. And I promise you this: The world, the church, and your very own family would be a drastically different place if we took this to heart.

THE MINEFIELD OF LIFE

As I was writing this book, the world I'm living in experienced an unprecedented crisis. If there weren't already enough issues facing the church, these past few years added a dozen more. I've watched churches split down the middle over who they've chosen to support, or how they've chosen to respond. I've watched families rent in two over opinions that have never had a discussion like this before in their lives. I've watched politics tear at the fabric of the church and ransack entire congregations and denominations. At this very moment, society is so tense that every conversation these days feels like walking through a minefield blindfolded.

I'm sure you've felt it. You never know which step could be your last.

This is where we need to hear Jesus's words—His reminder that a house divided against itself cannot stand. The enemy is trying to use each and every one of these issues to drive us apart—to divide and conquer. He's using them to lie to us and convince us that it is uniformity, not unity, that binds us together. That's his scheme, his plan.

This is a lie that binds: that if you don't agree with me, you're my enemy. We must remember that Jesus, with his blood, has bought and paid for not just our salvation, but our unity too! And he calls us to keep and defend that unity, not let it dissolve.

THE POWER OF A WEDGE

When it comes to division, I want you to look for this:

Fancy, isn't it? Not really, but hear me out. If you've never seen one of these before, it's called a splitting wedge. Maybe it doesn't look like much, or seem all that powerful, but you should see it in action. A little bit of force, a little bit of physics, and it's astonishing what this can do.

I first learned about these tools in a documentary I was watching on castle building in the Middle Ages. They were recreating how these massive limestone fortresses were built throughout Europe long before modern mining equipment. The stonemasons didn't have bulldozers, cranes, or diamond-tipped chainsaws. All they had were a few hammers and a handful of these wedges.

I watched the recreators at work, and they could mold, shape, and even split mammoth stone boulders with nothing more than a hammer and a small slender hunk of wedge-shaped iron like this. They would simply chip a few shallow holes in the face of a huge boulder, line them up, and drive a couple wedges in place. As hard as it might be to believe, they could split a hundred-ton boulder with one man, a hammer, and a dozen wedges—all by himself.

I remember watching this and being absolutely blown away. How can something so small cause so much damage? How can something so insignificant exert such power?

And the parallel hit.

This is what happens in the church when we let an open-handed issue become a wedge issue. This is what happens in our families and in our friendships when we let something small come between us—an errant word or a painful exchange. We hand the enemy one of these and say, "Here you go, try this!" We let him drive it in a little bit in the space between us.

He's ready, because he's been watching us all the time, looking for a hole. He's looking for some crack in our unity—some space to exploit. And we, with our petty issues and grievances, just hand him the wedge he's looking for.

Each time we bring it up, he drives it deeper. You can almost hear the sound of the hammer striking the wedge. *Ping.*

Every time we get worked up. *Ping.*

Every time we go, "Did you see what she was wearing last week? My goodness!" *Ping.*

"How many times have they already sung that song on a Sunday?" *Ping.*

"Did you hear what their kids did?" *Ping.*

On and on it goes, until one day you hear the boulder start to groan. From deep inside it begins to rumble, and before you know it, that huge rock fractures right down the fault line.

It seems sudden. It feels like it came out of nowhere, just like all division does. But I assure you, it didn't. The sounds have been ringing slow and steady with each and every swing.

I believe what Jesus is saying to all of us is this: "Stop giving him these!" Stop handing him shiny little wedges, and giving him the emotional energy he needs to drive them in.

When it comes to the true church, there's no us and them. There's just us. There are no sides. Remember, that the person across the aisle or across the street isn't the enemy. The enemy is not the person in the cubicle beside you, or in the house next door. You have an enemy—but they're not it. Your true enemy is doing everything he can to drive these wedges deeper until nothing remains.

Be watchful. Listen carefully. Pay attention when a relationship is becoming strained and begins to buckle. Listen closely when tensions are flaring and your church is starting to boil. Don't look in the directory, don't look in the news; look in the shadows. Listen for the sound of pinging. It's there, and it just might be what you need to realize who the real enemy is, and then rally the troops.

Remember the lie, and watch for it. Because if you don't agree with me, you are *not* my enemy.

5

The Lie of: Deception

Reality Isn't What God Told You
It Would Be

…When he lies, he speaks out of his own character,
for he is a liar and the father of lies.
JOHN 8:44B

I recently read an article that reminded me why modern art really isn't my thing. The article was about a "sculpture" (I use that term loosely) that sold at an art auction in France—and the sculpture is made of nothing. By that I don't mean it's insignificant, or hard to see; I mean it's literally made of *nothing*. It's invisible.

It's a piece by Salvatore Garau, an avant-garde Italian sculptor, and it fetched no less than $18,300 at the auction. In fact, there was a bidding war that began at $6,000 and continued climbing all the way to this ridiculous sum. Garau calls this creation an "immaterial sculpture" (which is to say it doesn't exist.) Have a look and you'll see what he means:

Perhaps you need an Italian accent to pull this off, but listen to how the sculptor describes it:

> The vacuum is nothing more than a space. Full of energy. And even if we empty it and there is nothing left, according to the Heisenberg uncertainty principle, that 'nothing' has a weight… Therefore it has energy that is condensed and transformed into particles… That is us.

If he can deliver that with a straight face, the man deserves an Oscar. The lucky buyer went home with a certificate of authenticity, a smile on his face, and a set of clear display instructions, including not to obstruct its view with any other object.

I can't be the only one who finds that ironic. "The Emperor Has No Clothes" must still be sitting unopened on his nightstand. And as it turns out, this wasn't Garau's only invisible sculpture—this was number two. He'd pulled this off twice!

After reading his story, I'm convinced Salvatore Garau has missed his true calling in life. With skills like his, he could have been a legendary marketing guru. The world would have been his oyster!

But even more than that, for me his story is a cautionary tale. It's a warning that we need to hear in this modern world now more than ever: *Be careful who you listen to.*

We tend to learn this lesson far too late in life. And when we finally do, it often comes at a hefty price. But who you trust will ultimately determine who you *become*—so choose carefully.

Deception at its root is the art of a lie. The word *deception* means to deceive, to misrepresent, or to mislead someone. In the end, it's always some kind of distortion of reality, a distortion that someone sold to you as truth. Whether it was at a used car lot where you bought your first car or at a French art auction, we've all experienced it before. And at its core we find one of the most dangerous lies we've been tricked into believing: *Reality isn't what God told us it would be.*

You can trace this lie back to the Bible's beginning. In fact, you might even say this was the very first lie ever told.

LIVING A LIE

A lie is a very dangerous thing. Once a lie is accepted—once we allow it into our souls, past our defenses—it unpacks like a malicious virus in the mainframe of our hearts and alters the very matrix of our lives.

Believe it or not, most of the power which the enemy wields in your life right now is rooted in his ability to get you to believe a lie and live like it's true. Let me show you what I mean.

Perhaps you were told at a young age that you won't amount to anything—that you don't matter. Instead of people speaking life into you as God designed them to, you've been told that you'll never aspire to much. It's not true. It's a lie from the pit of hell. But you've believed it and lived it each day like a self-fulfilling prophecy—afraid to reach too high.

Perhaps you've been told that some wrong choice you made years ago is really who you are. You've been told that your past is what defines you. That's not true, and yet you've believed it, and you've never been able to leave it behind. You've been forever chained to the mistakes you made, and you've dragged that identity into each and every relationship you've formed and every situation you've experienced.

Perhaps you've been told that what you achieve is who you are. You've been told that your identity is directly tied to your ability. This is one I struggle with deeply, and have since the age of five. My mother sat me down before my first day of kindergarten and told me not to worry about any of the other kids or about making friends, but to just do well in school and make the teacher happy. That was all that mattered, she said. It was one of those life-altering conversations that can change the course of your story. I have no clear memory of it; my mother first told me of our little chat twenty-five years later, and has apologized profusely ever since. But it set me up to believe that my identity was tied to what I could do and how well I could do it. Ever since, I have this driving need to accomplish things in life, and it's a switch I can't seem to turn off.

Sometimes that can feel like a thousand-pound weight on your shoulders. Perhaps like me, you've been led to believe that for other people to love and respect you, you must constantly be proving yourself and accomplishing great things. Again, that's not true! But you've believed it, and you've run yourself ragged for most of your life trying to keep up with the ghost of who you think you should be.

All these lies can propagate themselves and continue to affect you for decades. Unless, of course, you carefully delete the lie from the system code in your heart, and replace it with the truth.

One of my favorite examples comes out of Las Vegas. For many years, the marketing brain trust of Sin City used a slogan to lure people to visit. Its implications were immense. Maybe you recognize it: *Whatever happens in Vegas, stays in Vegas.*

Sound familiar? That line was plastered all over billboards and tv spots for almost a decade. It was everywhere, and the lie was clever. Here was the promise: Come to Vegas, let loose, blow off some steam—and don't worry about any repercussions. Nobody here knows you, no one will recognize you. You're in a consequence-free zone. Your bad decisions won't follow you home; they'll stay right here. So go wild!

Now let me ask you: Is that true? Do bad decisions stay in Vegas? Are consequences bound by state lines?

Of course not.

Does regret have a geographic statute of limitations?

Not on your life.

The truth is, people have picked up more baggage in Las Vegas than perhaps any other city in America and brought them home. But if you buy the lie—if you live like there's no tomorrow—then the damage is done. And when tomorrow comes, which it always does, it will bring along with it a whole bunch of our enemy's friends; remorse, regret, and consequence.

What we need to realize—and it's true of all the strategic lies of the enemy—is that the devil is a liar, and nothing he says can be trusted. Absolutely nothing. Remember what Jesus said about him:

> He was a murderer from the beginning, not holding to the truth, for there is no truth in him. When he lies, he speaks his native language, for he is a liar and the father of lies. (John 8:44)

I don't think Jesus could have been clearer. *There is no truth in him.* Our enemy is a silver-tongued salesman—a con man. He's a grifter and a charlatan. He sells snake oil on the corner of every street, and disappears the next day. Once you realize this, it weakens his spell. Each and every day, he's trying to lie to you, because when he lies he speaks his native language. It's all he knows how to do.

To borrow the immortal words of Meghan Trainor: If his lips are movin', then he's lyin', lyin', lyin'.

NEVER DINE WITH THE DEVIL

Our first parents got a crash course in deception, and their story is another cautionary tale. It's about the shocking power of a lie. Eve back then made two critical mistakes in rapid succession, and it shook the very foundations of the created order. See if you can spot the two lies.

Now the serpent was more crafty than any of the wild animals the Lord God had made. He said to the woman, "Did God really say, 'You must not eat from any tree in the garden'?"

The woman said to the serpent, "We may eat fruit from the trees in the garden, but God did say, 'You must not eat fruit from the tree that is in the middle of the garden, and you must not touch it, or you will die.'"

"You will not certainly die," the serpent said to the woman. "For God knows that when you eat from it your eyes will be opened, and you will be like God, knowing good and evil."

When the woman saw that the fruit of the tree was good for food and pleasing to the eye, and also desirable for gaining wisdom, she took some and ate it. She also gave some to her husband, who was with her, and he ate it. Then the eyes of both of them were opened, and they realized they were naked; so they sewed fig leaves together and made coverings for themselves. (Genesis 3:1-7)

If you've grown up in church, you've heard this story many times. I know I did. I can still see the flannelgraph Eve and the garden full of trees. We think we know the story from the sheer amount of exposure, but we often miss crucial details about their interaction and the battle taking place. Regardless of how you read this section of Scripture, it's a foundational story of the Christian worldview. Upon it rests the entire weight of the gospel story, and if you're ever wondering why the world is the way it is—beautiful and broken simultaneously—this is it. This is why you can be awed by a brilliant sunrise one day, then running from a hurricane the next. This world is both beautiful and broken because it was made good, then marred by sin. But the narrative in Genesis tells us more than just how things began. It's also a story about how a lie can cost us everything. So pay attention—there will be moments when you and I face the identical trap.

Usually we assume that Eve's first mistake was taking a bite of the apple, but the story is far more layered than that. When you recreate the ancient garden battle and retrace their steps, it turns out that this interaction is far closer to the end than the beginning. As you watch the story develop, you soon realize there were countless things happening here long before the climax. (By the way, this is by no means an attempt to pick on Eve alone. Scripture is clear that Adam was standing there right beside her for much of the time, and on the whole he was just as culpable as she was. They did this together).

In this story, Eve was set up—no doubt about it. But in the final analysis, it's also true that she allowed herself to be.

DON'T TALK TO HIM

Like I said, we assume her first mistake was taking a bite of the apple, but her first error in this battle came long before. Her first mistake was getting into a conversation with the serpent in the first place.

Let me give you a little advice. If you're ever walking down the street, minding your own business, and a snake begins to speak to you from one of the nearby trees...*run!* Run as fast and as far as you can. Run until your legs won't carry you anymore. Run like your life depends on it. You may think this is common sense, but how often do we get into a conversation with temptation before we realize it's too late? The truth is, nothing good will ever come from a dialogue like this.

When has a story you wanted to live ever started with the words "Then the snake said..."? There was an early window of escape that she missed. God promises us that he will always provide a way out of temptation (1 Corinthians 10:13), but sometimes that off-ramp is right at the beginning.

If Eve had kept walking, none of the lies—and none of the deception—would have had time to take root. Deception is like a heavy fog; it takes time to roll in. Engaging in a conversation like this gave the enemy all the space he needed to spin his web of lies and lure her into a trap.

The first takeaway from Eve's story is this: *Don't talk to him.* That's how we get into trouble.

We have a rule in our house. If a salesman ever comes to our door, I'm the one who does the talking. My wife is tremendously loving and caring, and one of the sweetest people you'll ever meet. You would like her, I can guarantee it. Absolutely everyone does. But she hates conflict. It's her kryptonite.

There's virtually nothing she despises more than making people feel uncomfortable. More than once I've marched into a clothing store and returned multiple women's garments because she would rather keep them than face the cashier. I don't mind in the least, although the judgmental stares tend to sting a bit.

So when salesmen would come to our door, often my wife would invite them right in. They were shown the couch and given the red carpet treatment. We made this rule after she invited a frozen meat salesman into our house to give us an hour-long sales pitch on overpriced unmarked meat. The whole hour I was glaring at her. My eyes simply said, "*Why?* Why did you do this to me? What have I ever done to deserve this? Have I offended you in some way? Is this some form of punishment?" I was simply biding my time until I kicked him out. Now, whether it's meat salesmen or timeshare reps, I'm the one who answers the door to send them packing. Why?

Because nothing good will ever come of it.

I believe we need to make that rule with the enemy. When temptation comes knocking, and that thought pops into your head, don't have a conversation with it. Don't consider it. Don't start weighing out the pros and cons. The minute you start making that kind of list, you're already in grave danger. Don't start contemplating if you should have that second or third or sixth piece of cake. Don't consider whether sneaking out at night to go to a party is worth the risk—this is always how it begins.

Don't talk to him. Nothing good will ever come of it. All you're doing is giving the enemy space to spin.

I think that most of us, deep down inside, naively think that we're strong enough to hear the devil out and smart enough to outwit him. There's nothing our culture loves more than options, and we want to at least hear his pitch. But we underestimate the power of the siren's song. We forget that Jesus was the only one who was able to stand up to all temptation and walk away victorious. There's a reason we were taught never to play with fire.

DON'T TRUST HIM

But there was a second mistake in this exchange between Eve and the serpent. It came shortly after her first blunder. Eve's second fundamental error was the fact that she trusted him. If you read the serpent's words to Eve carefully, you'll see how he bends and twists the truth. He plays fast and loose with the words God had already spoken. First he plants doubt in Eve's heart that God really said what she thought he said. "Did God really say…?" He's been using that question ever since, and it's been echoing in the hallways of so many of our churches today.

Then he twists God's instructions to include every tree in Eden, when God roped off only one. Instead of the one central tree God has fenced off for Adam and Eve's safety, the serpent implies that it was all of the trees. He insinuates that God doesn't want them to touch *any* tree in this beautiful forest.

Then, with his hook set deep, he comes right out and tells Eve that God didn't really mean what he said—that God was lying to her.

Ironic, no?

He drops the veil, and attempts the full-strength, high-test, unabashed lie: *God is holding out on you*. If Eve had her wits about her, she would have questioned the very premise. She would never have believed him; she would have known that God would never do anything like that. To paraphrase G. K. Chesterton: "Never take down a fence until you know why it was put there in the first place."[7]

Once you start to push past the fog and mirrors, you get a sense of what the serpent was doing. He was framing God. It was deception, pure and simple. He was painting him as a cosmic killjoy. A cop on a power trip. Restrictive. Unreasonable. Repressive. He was telling Eve that God didn't really want what was best for her (sound familiar?). And her lethal mistake was believing this lie.

Sadly, Adam and Eve paid the ultimate price. We all did. Their soul shriveled and died within them, and they were kicked out of paradise. The consequences of their choice have been reverberating through history ever since. They lost everything, all because they trusted a liar.

TESTING WITH TRUTH

Make no mistake, deception is a very effective tool. The spell it casts is very hard to break, and when you're in its grip, it's hard to know which way is up. It's like an avalanche that thoroughly spins and buries you; you're desperate to dig out, but you can't figure out which way leads to sunlight.

The people you know who are caught in this deception are caught in more than a single untruth; they're caught in a web of lies. Eve was so disoriented, she did the singular thing God had commanded her not to do. If she'd only caught her breath and centered her thoughts, she would have discerned what to do. The same is true for you and me when we sense the enemy's call. So don't talk to him, don't trust him, and when you're unsure, test everything with truth. This is exactly what Jesus did when he faced the devil in the desert. Each of the devil's lies was cut apart by the living, breathing, truth from the Word of God.

There's an interesting parallel in the world of counterfeit money, a modern day catch-me-if-you-can. Federal agents are trained to spot falsified checks and counterfeit bills, but not in the way you might think. They don't study forgeries and signature signs of each counterfeit artist. They're almost exclusively trained by studying the real thing. They spend time poring over what a real dollar bill looks like, feels like, and smells like. They stare endlessly at how it reflects the light. They pay attention to the texture under their finger and how it bends and folds then snaps back. They spend so much time studying the real thing that when they're exposed to a forgery, it's instantly apparent. It sticks out like a sore thumb.

This is why we spend so much time studying the Word of God. It's the truth. The real thing. It's the standard by which all things are judged, the atomic clock by which every timepiece is set. God's Word is "alive and active. Sharper than any double-edged sword, it penetrates even to dividing soul and spirit, joints and marrow" (Hebrews 4:12). Anything that doesn't match, we know is an impostor.

These days, vices are dressed like virtues. Temptation masquerades as self-care. Sometimes Paul tells us the enemy even dresses in angelic white. We must be on our guard—now more than ever.

So what do we watch for? How do we spot deception? We refuse to allow it any time and space to warp our vision of reality. We refuse to give it room to spin. We do exactly what the federal agents do, and compare it with the real thing.

HISSING S'S

Here's another way to think of this. I've preached this to my congregation for years. You must listen for the *hissing s's*.

There's an animated classic that retells the tale of Robin Hood. If you have kids, you've probably seen it more times than you can count. It's the same familiar story, translated for a pint-sized audience.

There's a fascinating character in this adaptation named Hiss. He's a snake—a talking snake at that, and an adviser to the king. He constantly sits beside the king and gives him advice about how to rule. He's ever present, always at his shoulder, and every time he speaks, he hisses his s's. Every other part of his speech is normal, but his s's always hiss.

"Yessss, Ssssire…" "That soundssss like a fabuloussss plan…" You can identify him with your eyes closed. When my kids were watching the show, I could pick him out from the next room.

If you listen carefully to the things our culture says, and the thoughts that emerge in your head—if you're willing to slow down and concentrate and invite God into that moment, you'll hear the hiss.

Deception always has a tell.

It may seem altogether right and true, but if you're willing to listen, some people's s's will hiss. Something will seem out of place. There'll be a glitch in the matrix. You'll have a gut feeling, deep in your spirit, that something's amiss.

We'll talk more about that feeling later. Meanwhile, make the commitment to listen to that voice. Listen for the hissing s's. Call it out when you hear it. God just may be trying to save you from a well-laid trap.

6

The Lie of: **Fear**

Your Situation Is Bigger than God

Be strong and courageous. Do not be afraid or
terrified because of them, for the Lord your God goes
with you; he will never leave you nor forsake you.
DEUTERONOMY 31:6

A few years after we were married, Mel and I started hearing unusual sounds coming from inside the walls of our house. It was a faint, almost scratching sound emanating from behind the plaster. It was so quiet that unless all the kids were asleep, and the TV was switched off, and everyone was sitting still, you couldn't hear it. But every once in a while, you would hear the scratching. I don't need to tell you how unnerving that was.

That setup sounds like the beginning of some thriller movie, and it felt like it too. Even more unusual, the sound moved. One day it was upstairs in the bathroom. The next it was beside the kitchen. Eventually it even migrated to more interior walls. I would come home and Mel would say, "Shhhh! Listen!"

Born and raised in the city, I had no idea what to do with this. Was it a mouse? A possum? A squirrel? A family of chipmunks? Your guess was as good as mine. I was just about to call an exterminator, but in the end it proved unnecessary. We found out exactly what was making the noise. Late one night, just as we were about to turn out the lights and head to bed, a bat climbed out of one of the vents and started flying around the living room.

Bats terrify me—and I'm not too proud to admit it. I have no idea why, but I have a deep irrational fear of those little flying rodents. I can't point to a day or time when this began, or to some vicious childhood memory that sparked it, but there's just something about them that makes my skin crawl. Maybe it's because they're so silent when they fly—it's just unnatural. Maybe it's their leathery wings or their beady little eyes. Or maybe I just watched too many vampire movies when I was a kid. For whatever reason, bats are like kryptonite for me. Whenever one is nearby, I picture it flying into my face, and my having to slowly peel it off.

That night when the bat emerged from the vent, I did what any man of the house would do. I ran out of the living room as fast as I could and left my wife to fend for herself. After a few minutes of painful silence, I told her I was regrouping and coming up with a plan, but we both knew I was lying through my teeth. Mel on the other hand put me to shame and stood her ground against our flying intruder.

No matter what, I couldn't talk myself into going back in. I was stuck. I kept telling myself: "You're a grown man! It's a tiny little bat! You're a hundred times its size! March right back in there." But the pep talk didn't work. I was frozen. So in a moment of sheer genius, I grabbed a tall laundry basket, threw it over my head, and hung on for dear life! Safe under my plastic bat shield, I emerged in the living room. Mel just looked at me. She didn't say anything. She didn't have to. The look on her face spoke volumes all on its own.

There I was, standing in my living room with a laundry basket over my head, while my wife was tracking down the bat and trying to trap it in a blanket. Hey, you want equal rights? There they are.

Sure enough, a few minutes later, Mel yelled, "I got it!" I was more than a little surprised. I walked over, not ready to take off the hamper until I was sure of my safety, and there was the blanket, on the floor, with a little lump in it. Realizing my chance to be her knight in shining armor was disappearing fast, I took off my basket, tightly gathered up the blanket, and took it outside.

I don't need to tell you this wasn't exactly my finest hour. Having your wife save you from a six-inch flying rodent doesn't do much for your self-esteem. I comfort myself with the fortunate reality that no photographs of this event were taken. But when it was all over, I asked her the question burning a hole in my chest. "Weren't you scared?"

She said, "Of course I was. But I wasn't about to be up all night, so I took care of it."

Right.

I learned a lot that night. A lot about what real courage looks like. Courage isn't what we often assume. Her answer was perfect. Of course she was afraid, but she wasn't about to let that fear rule her life.

We usually think courage is for people who don't feel fear. But it isn't. Courage isn't the absence of fear; it is forward motion in the face of fear.

I also learned a lot about fear, about what it feels like, what it does to the soul. Not all fears are as trivial as the one I faced that night. Not all of them are so easily dealt with. But they all *feel* very much the same. Fear is visceral. It originates deep in your gut. Sometimes it's overwhelming.

Many of our fears are irrational. Apparently more than 85 percent of the things we worry over never happen anyway, and of the 15 percent that do, 79 percent of those situations turn out more positive in scope than we feared.[8] Reading those numbers blew me away. Our fears don't obey logic, and they rarely respond to pep talks or motivational speeches. They're a monster built from all the what-ifs and remote possibilities that will likely never occur. Fear doesn't respond to logic because it was never logical to begin with. You can't argue someone out of something they were never argued into in the first place.

Fear can be immobilizing. I remember when our first child was born. Everything went according to plan. Well, maybe not everything, but after twelve hours of labor I was standing there in the hospital room holding my son for the first time and smiling at my wife. It was amazing. Then my wife's eyes started to close. All of a sudden the nurses rushed back in, and started yelling instructions at each other in clipped sentences. It all happened so fast. The doctor flew into the room, and there was more blood than I'd ever seen in my life. The doctor kept yelling, "Stay awake, Mel, stay with us." I stood there completely frozen, wondering if I was watching the love of my life slip away while holding my brand new son. I'd never been so scared in my life.

Fear rivets you to the floor wherever you're standing; it refuses to let you move. It's a club the enemy wields to keep us at bay. If temptation is an attempt to draw you off the path God has called you down, fear is an attempt to drive you off it. And many times in our lives, it works. When we respond in fear rather than faith, we're letting a lie shape the course of our lives.

There's a subtle lie baked into each and every one of the fears we face: *This is bigger than God.* That same fiction lies beneath all the fears and worries we struggle with.

I don't know what *this* is for you right now; it could be a job loss, or a medical diagnosis, or your son or daughter heading off to college for their freshman year. It could be financial pressure that won't let up, or a goal you've pursued that seems to be falling apart. Whatever situation you're facing right now, there's a lie the enemy will whisper in your ear as you try to fall asleep at night: "This is bigger than the God you serve." No attempt to conquer the fears and worries we struggle with in our lives will be successful until we confront this lie.

Think of how many opportunities in life you never took advantage of because you were afraid of how they might turn out. Think of how many relationships you never pursued because fear held you back. Think of how many decisions you made on the basis of fear rather than on the basis of hope.

We need to recognize that these anxieties and fears trace their source to a spring much deeper than just our own ruminations. Fear has a spiritual root, and any attempt to cut that weed above the surface alone will never truly be effective. A spiritual problem requires a spiritual solution.

So what makes fear so dangerous? There are two fundamental reasons.

FEAR PARALYZES YOU

I can still picture myself crouching in the other room, willing myself to go back where the bat was, but simply unable to overcome the barrier. You know what that feels like don't you? Fear is paralyzing. It immobilizes you. It rivets you to the spot, unable to move. You can't progress forward. Sometimes you can't even retreat. You can't grow. You get stuck in a rut where you are. It's like you're in spiritual quicksand.

All fear functions like this. Fear of commitment will freeze you right where you're at in your relationships—never able to move forward. Fear renders future progress impossible, because progress requires partnership. Fear of what other people think (what the Bible calls the fear of man) will freeze you right where you are in life, never able to step out into something greater. It leaves you in a constant state of worry that you'll offend someone with a choice you make. It ices you and blocks any progress in your relationship with God, because you're more concerned about what your friends think than what God thinks.

Fear of stepping out of your comfort zone will keep you from trying new things and growing through new experiences.

This kind of fear will cost you the joys of growth. Fear of losing someone you love almost robs you of the time you actually have left.

Each and every time, fear functions the same. It freezes you right where you are. This lie that whatever you're facing is bigger than God is like a ball and chain you drag around with you everywhere you go.

FEAR PREOCCUPIES YOU

When you're afraid of something, often it's all you can think about. I would imagine this is more than familiar to us all. It's the engine that drives all the worry that plagues our minds and our hearts. It robs you of your peace deep inside.

There's a small part of the brain called the amygdala that's dedicated to assessing any present danger in the situations we're in. The amygdala is small, but don't let its size fool you; it's tremendously powerful. It's the part of your brain that lights up when you meet an unsuspecting bear on a hike, or hear a rattlesnake's rattle on the ground nearby. This small region of the brain is what sends us into fight or flight mode; and it sometimes locks us in that frame of mind when we see a threat.

My son had a bad experience with water as a toddler. He fell face down in the shallows of a lake with a life jacket on, and couldn't stand back up. It was only twelve inches of water, but it changed his life. One of the other moms nearby had to grab him by the jacket and pull him up because he was thrashing around a cat in a bathtub, unable to regain his footing. He was so terrified he swore off swimming for life.

I could understand his hesitation, but it wasn't just when we were by the water that he thought about it. He thought about it all the time, day and night. He would come to me late some evenings and say, "Dad, you can't make me swim!" He would say it defiantly and repeatedly, as if I'd been nagging him all afternoon about swimming—when we hadn't talked about it even once all day. Yet it was still the song constantly playing on repeat in his mind.

How ironic that in the process of trying to get away from something, we end up bound to it! Fear preoccupies you with the very thing you're trying to get away from, and leaves room for little else.

FEAR NOT!

Did you know that the most common command in the Bible is "Fear not"? It has been said that in Scripture this command occurs 365 times in some form or another—one for every single day of the year. I wasn't able to substantiate this claim, since it depends on how wide you spread the net, but even the more conservative estimates place it in the hundreds. Remarkable, isn't it? There are literally hundreds of situations in Scripture where God's first words to us are, "Fear not!" Each time it comes as a command, not a suggestion.

In those instances when I sense fear creeping into my heart and seeping into my soul, I'm often drawn to Paul's words to Timothy: "For God did not give you a spirit of fear, but of power, love, and a sound mind" (2 Timothy 1:7 NKJV).

I love that. I've memorized it and used it on countless occasions. I actually carried it around in my back pocket for years, and pulled it out every time I felt fear knocking on the door of my heart. The word "fear" here in Greek is *deilia*. It means cowardice or fearfulness. It's not referring to terror that comes in an emergency, or caution that comes from respecting something that's genuinely dangerous—there's a different Greek word for both of those. *Deilia* means regularly being pushed around, shrinking back, hiding behind something.

God has called us to a brave and bold abundant life. I believe that with all my heart. Fear is the polar opposite to what he has called us to. We let fear hold us hostage, to bully us and push us around.

And did you notice that Paul doesn't just call it fear, but a *spirit* of fear? Why? Because fear fundamentally has a spiritual root.

SPIRITUAL SIGHT

There's a thrilling story in 2 Kings in which the prophet Elisha found himself on the bad side of the king of Aram. For a long time, Elisha had been thwarting the king's ambushes and surprise attacks, making life miserable for him. So the king made plans to hunt down the prophet.

> "Go, find out where he is," the king ordered, "so I can send men and capture him." The report came back: "He is in Dothan." Then he sent horses and chariots and a strong force there. They went by night and surrounded the city.
>
> When the servant of the man of God got up and went out early the next morning, an army with horses and chariots had surrounded the city. "Oh no, my lord! What shall we do?" the servant asked.
>
> "Don't be afraid," the prophet answered. "Those who are with us are more than those who are with them."
>
> And Elisha prayed, "Open his eyes, Lord, so that he may see." Then the Lord opened the servant's eyes, and he looked and saw the hills full of horses and chariots of fire all around Elisha. (2 Kings 6:13-17)

I don't know what your threshold for fear is, but I'm fairly sure this would cross the line. Imagine you went to bed one night, and when you awoke the next morning and grabbed your coffee, you looked out the window to see an entire army surrounding your house—not just a soldier or two, or a gang of thugs, but a horde of infantry armed to the teeth, fully positioned around your property—their swords glinting in the sunlight.

Talk about terrifying! Imagine the adrenaline that must have coursed through the veins of Elisha's servant as he stared across the yard. This is what he awoke to.

He ran back inside, breathless and petrified, and relayed the situation to his master. But Elisha, cool as ever, told him not to be afraid. (There's that command again.) Then he told him why: "Those who are with us are more than those who are with them."

What a cryptic line. I bet his servant went back to the window and had another look, feeling certain his master had lost his mind. He did a quick recount. It didn't take long. The enemy had a multitude, an entire national army too numerous to count. But on Elisha's side, they had one, two. Two people. That's it. Two men who didn't even own a sword.

Then Elisha prayed that God would open his servants' eyes. That's a key line in the story. Apparently the servant's fear was rooted in an inability to see clearly. His fear was intricately tied to what he was focused on. Once God opened his eyes, however, he saw the hills full of horses and chariots of fire! Man, that must have been a sight! The host of heaven, spread across the hillside, armed and ready for battle! I have no idea what a chariot of fire would look like, but I would give just about anything to find out.

In that moment, everything changed. In that one instant, all the fears that Elisha's servant was wrestling with evaporated and melted away. Why? Because he saw with his own eyes that God was bigger than their situation.

The lie he'd been holding in his heart was broken in an instant. No matter how big this situation was, it wasn't bigger than God! Elisha was surrounded by an army, but that army was itself surrounded by a host of God's angelic warriors.

PRESENT AND POWERFUL

Neil Anderson writes that in order for fear to be activated, the object we fear must possess two things: presence and power.[9] On their own, neither is enough. Fear arises from things that are *both* imminently present and objectively powerful.

Take snakes, for example. In the Amazon, some snakes grow up to thirty feet long. They're a terrifying sight. These boa constrictors are powerful enough to choke the life out of a full grown man in a matter of hours—tightening their grip after each and every breath.

Now, were you thinking of snakes before you read this paragraph? Were you actively looking around your feet for one? Probably not. But aren't snakes powerful? Of course they are, but you know they're not immediately present. Those boa constrictors are powerful, but they're thousands of miles away in a jungle you don't plan to set foot in, so you aren't afraid.

Now, let's alter the setting. Adjust the context. Imagine you found a huge python in your bed at night. Would you be afraid? I know, silly question. You'd be terrified, because all of a sudden they're both powerful and present, in a horrifying way.

The same holds true for a lamb. Take that scenario and swap out the intruder. If you were wakened at three in the morning by a stray sheep that had wandered into your bedroom—you would be surprised, but likely not afraid. They might even help you get back to sleep if there were enough of them to count. You wouldn't be afraid because the sheep is present but not powerful.

So both of those ingredients are necessary for fear to exist. They're the elemental building blocks of fear. The army that Elisha's servant saw out the window was both immediately present and remarkably powerful. But why wasn't Elisha himself afraid? There's the million dollar question. Why was Elisha so relaxed? That same army was surrounding him too.

Elisha wasn't afraid because even though that army was both present and powerful, they were no match for the God he served, who was infinitely greater. The armies of heaven were far more present and wildly more powerful! Innumerable and immeasurable! And that vastly superior army of that vastly superior God was there guarding him.

Seeing and understanding that disarmed the fear that was trying to grip Elisha's heart. The lie no longer held any power over him.

Elisha walked out his front door without an ounce of fear. He greeted the army, prayed that God would strike them with blindness, then led them by the hand into an Israelite fortress. He used some sort of Spirit-led Jedi mind trick and convinced them that he wasn't the man they were looking for, but that he would lead them straight to him if they followed along.

What army is surrounding you right now? It may be a different one than showed up last year or last month. You may be dealing with a fear of failure, unable to move forward because you're afraid it's all going to come crashing down like it did last time. You may be facing a medical challenge; the doctor's report didn't come back the way you'd hoped; that diagnosis is staring you in the face, with a six-letter word burned into your thoughts. Or you may be dealing with fear for your kids, as every parent has felt—fear for their safety, or about their character development, or about the future that's so very unknown. The army threatening you might be financial pressure that seems impossible to overcome, and you can't possibly see a way out; its vice-like grip seems to strengthen with every week.

The enemy will try to intimidate you with whatever he can! He'll lie to you about all the ways this can go wrong. He'll fill you with worry and fear, and he'll replay an endless set of negative possibilities. He'll whisper that this is bigger than the God you serve, and he'll show up at your place with a squadron of his soldiers to try and turn you around.

But don't be afraid. It's a mirage.

"Those who are with us are more than those who are with them..."

In those moments, we need a refresher, an instantaneous reminder of a promise God makes—that he who is in you is greater than he who is in the world. It was the apostle John who taught us this:

> You, dear children, are from God and have overcome them, because the one who is in you is greater than the one who is in the world. (1 John 4:4)

So long as we believe that the threat in front of us is greater than the Spirit inside us, our hands will shake and our knees will buckle. But once we realize that when God is for us, no one can be against us, it awakens an irrepressible surge of life-altering faith. It's an overflowing spring. We need not fear the army in front of us, because the God inside us is greater.

THE DISPLACEMENT PRINCIPLE

In my experience, fear isn't ultimately coaxed away; rather, it's *displaced*. We often try to drive our fears out with platitudes and motivational posters. We try to think our way through it, or distract ourselves from it. Sometimes we self-medicate. But ultimately this fear is a spiritual problem and requires a spiritual solution. We must stand our ground and refuse to bow to the threats it makes. Fear isn't something we can talk ourselves out of, because we're surrounded by things we cannot control, and which may potentially cause us harm. The fear must be displaced.

Think of a bowl filled with air. What's the easiest way to remove the air from inside it? The engineer and scientist might tell you that if you create a vacuum with sufficient pressure you can suck the air right out, leaving a void in its place. The philosopher might question what we mean by air and space. But they're all overthinking it. The easiest way to remove the air is to fill the bowl with something else.

No matter what the enemy is trying to intimate you with, and no matter how powerful or present it may seem, you must remember that nothing is more powerful or present than God.

Nothing.

There's no force in all the cosmos more powerful or more present than he is. He's omnipotent—which means power without measure, and unlimited control. And he's omnipresent—which means he is everywhere, including inside and beside you as you read this. Both of these are fundamental attributes of the living God. Nothing is more powerful or present than God.

We can know this, with profound awareness. The Bible often speaks of this awareness as *the fear of God*. It's not a cowering type of fear, but awesome reverence and respect. It's the awareness of who he truly is. So you must allow him to occupy the space your fear used to in your heart. Allow God himself to displace it.

You must fill your mind with those reminders. Renew your mind with these truths. God is large and in charge. He's in control—sovereign over all things. No one can take that away from him. And he loves you with all his heart.

It may look like you're surrounded—but never forget, you're surrounded by *him*. Pray like Elisha did—that God would open your eyes. Those who are with you are more than those who are with them.

What should you watch for? What do we keep our eyes open to see? Soldiers. Messengers of intimidation. The things that knock on the door of your heart and don't stop, and thoughts that revisit you night after night. Once you see the uniform, and the threats they bring, remember this story. Ask God to open your eyes.

7

The Lie of: **Accusation**

You Are Who Others Say You Are

Who will bring a charge against God's elect?
God is the one who justifies...
Romans 8:33

They seem to have gone out of style as of late, but when I grew up, name tags were everywhere—those small white stickers that said something like "Hello, my name is..." with a blank space below to write your name.

First day of school, business conferences, meet-and-greets, summer camp—wherever there were new faces, name tags were there to break the ice. Of course, the best part about them was that what you wrote was up to you. Whether it was your full name, your nickname, your initials, or your favorite superhero—this was your chance to tell this room full of strangers who you were or who you wanted to be.

Now I know that doesn't sound all that profound at face value, and maybe you've never given it a moment's thought. But it was actually a powerful exercise.

Names are powerful.

In the Bible, names were an encapsulation of who you were, and often became a prophecy of the life you would come to live. The name Moses for example means "to be drawn out of the water." It was a beautiful testimony to the way God rescued him from the clutches of murderous soldiers, pulled him from the river, and planted him right in Pharaoh's household. It was his life story, retold every time someone called his name. Each time a friend in the palace called for him, or God spoke to him from the mountain, he heard this: "You are the one God drew out of the water."

For all of us, actually, names are a fundamental part of our identity.

Growing up, it doesn't take long to realize that you're not the only one who tries to fill in that blank space. It turns out that other people will often try to do it for you. They'll speak things over you. Label you. Attempt to define you and tell you who you are.

As a grade school student, I was in Mr. Antoniak's class. One day he selected me to write the homework on the blackboard for that afternoon. It doesn't sound like an overly auspicious job, but it was a huge honor in his class. For a teacher's pet, this was about as good as it gets. He tried to tell me how he wanted it written, but I just couldn't get it. Three or four times he explained what he wanted me to write, but I continued to scribe it wrong.

Looking back, I believe he wanted me to indent the next line, and continue writing. It sounds simple, but he never quite said it that way. Just before I sat down, he spoke something over me that I've never quite been able to forget. It was one of those sentences that followed me around for years. He said, "You know what, Chris? You're a smart kid, but you have no common sense."

He said it only once, but I must have heard it a thousand times. His statement was matter of fact. I'm convinced he meant nothing by it. There was no malice nor malevolence in his voice. But he said it right in front of a classroom full of my peers, and it sunk deeply into my identity.

Pivotal moments don't always feel like it at the time. It's not like in the movies. There's no ominous music swelling in the background. There's no external indication that your life's about to change.

I didn't realize it as it happened, but that stuck with me—that label. It profoundly impacted how I saw myself for years to come. Somehow it became a part of me. I'd assimilated it just like all the other characteristics of who I was, and I assumed Mr. Antoniak was right: I could tackle the hard things in life, but the simple stuff was too much. I had no common sense.

I carried that label for years. It would be a full decade before I finally ripped it off.

It's sad, but time and again that's how we acquire parts of our identity. Someone will say something about you—speak something over you—and it will stick. A friend or family member will label us, and it becomes a part of how we see ourselves. We start to form our identity from the labels we've picked up along the way.

Now I know that what Mr. Antoniak said about me was not the worst label a person can wear. In the sum total of my life, I'm sure I've been called worse. I think most of us have. But in that moment, something rather deep was happening in that room— something that has also happened to you. In that moment, someone stuck a label to my chest and walked away, possibly forever changing my identity.

Do you remember the rhyme we grew up saying? "Sticks and stones may break my bones but words will never hurt?" I heard it every week in grade school, and I still hear my kids saying it decades later. What that saying lacked in truth it made up for in persistence. I'm convinced there has never been a lie more readily repeated than this one. This tactic of identity reassignment is more than just a schoolyard game. It has tremendous capacity to affect the trajectory of our lives.

If you can change how people view themselves, you can alter their destiny.

Read that sentence again. Nothing about it is an exaggeration. We make decisions in life based on who we think we are. We live out of our identity. Often we assume it's the other way around. We assume our activity defines our identity—that our actions define who we are. But Scripture repeatedly teaches that the opposite is true. Once you understand who you are, you'll start to live like it.

When I was ten years old, I made cardboard wings and jumped off our garage. I don't know where my parents were, but wherever it was, it wasn't close enough. I'd watched too many cartoons, which blurred the line for me between fantasy and reality. I figured if I just flapped hard enough, I would achieve liftoff. My little brother followed right behind me. I thought I could fly, so I challenged gravity. It was that simple. I was living out of my identity. See, my actions followed my convictions about myself. As you may have guessed, I was wrong that day about who I was. I fell from the sky like a lead balloon. My strength-to-weight ratio was nowhere near enough to fly, and physics resolutely turned against me.

On a more serious note, my father struggled with self-worth his entire life. For some reason that no one could identify, he never really believed he deserved anything good in his life. It was heartbreaking to watch, but he always found a way to sabotage the good things that God brought his way. He lived out the identity he thought was true of him. He was fired from a handful of great jobs for the most unusual reasons. Once he quit an excellent job with an outstanding company, only to land once again in a cutthroat business that churned him up and spit him out. It was hard to watch, but it was this truth with flesh on. He didn't believe he deserved anything good, and he lived out that conviction every chance he was given.

We live out of our identity. That's the power inherent in the words we use. It's why God repeatedly exhorts us in Scripture to speak life. Here's the reason: "The tongue has the power of life and death" (Proverbs 18:21). I've spent years trying to practice that one proverb, especially with my kids—because I know how lasting an impact my words will have on them.

This is why so much of Scripture is there to solidify your understanding of who you are as a child of the King, and it's why identity is such an overarching theme. This is why Paul calls the people in the Corinthian church *saints* even though their lives are far from reflecting that truth. When you read 1 Corinthians, you can't help but wonder if Paul forgot who he was writing to when he penned that introduction. Why did he still call them saints if he was going to spend the next fourteen chapters correcting their mistakes?

Why? Because those words are literally shaping the hearts, minds, and realities of the people around us every day. They're that powerful. Paul was building into them the truth they needed to live out their calling.

So it's no accident I still remember a single sentence a grade school teacher spoke to me thirty years ago.

So speak life. Speak truth. Life and death truly do hang in the balance.

The lie we come to believe—sometimes through no fault of our own—is that we are who others say we are. We believe we're different people from the ones God made us to be. We believe those labels that have been stuck to our chest by the people in our story. Through the reckless words of others and the careless thoughts in our head, those lies begin to alter our identity.

The truth is, *our identity determines our destiny.*

It's worthwhile to stop here for a moment and ask yourself: What labels have others stuck to you? Which ones have you carried without ever questioning if they were right? Perhaps it was from a friend or a schoolmate, or a parent early in your life. If you can identify the labels and trace them back to their source, this will begin to break the power they've held over you all these years. Take a moment to reflect on this, and ask the Holy Spirit to guide you.

I've counseled countless people who struggle with a low self-esteem and a warped understanding of their identity. I fight through some of those lies myself on a weekly basis. In this struggle, the problem for most of us is that we don't know who we really are. We don't know our true identity in Christ. So many followers of Jesus don't know what God has said about them, or about the stunningly rich inheritance that came with the Spirit who now lives inside them.

Ultimately that's how we'll win this war. Not just by rejecting the lies we've been told, but by accepting the truth about who God has made us to be. *Identify, trace, replace*—that same rhythm is what will lead us to freedom. We must remove those false labels that have been illegitimately placed, and replace them with the truth God has spoken over us in his Word.

THE ACCUSER

Revelation is a book full of unforgettable scenes. As a kid with an overactive imagination, I was drawn to it like a moth to a flame. Of the many vivid pictures, one that has often held my imagination for years relates to our identity. Listen to what the apostle John experienced:

Then I heard a loud voice in heaven say: "Now have come the salvation and the power and the kingdom of our God, and the authority of his Messiah. For the accuser of our brothers and sisters, who accuses them before our God day and night, has been hurled down. They triumphed over him by the blood of the Lamb and by the word of their testimony." (Revelation 12:10-11)

There's a lot going on in these few verses. It's a picture of our final victory over the enemy, and our marching orders on how to arrive there. But the fundamental picture of this passage is a courtroom. In this scene, the enemy is the Accuser (one of the devil's many titles in Scripture). And did you catch what he was doing each and every day? Actually, not just every day but every night as well. He is accusing us before God who sits on his throne.

Pleasant thought, isn't it?

Day and night he stands before God and accuses us of all the wrong things we've ever done.

"Accuser" in Greek is the word *diablos*. It's where we get the word *diabolical*. It means slanderer or someone who makes false accusations. Revelation tells us that day and night, Satan stands before God and makes accusations about you and me.

The enemy says, "God, didn't you see what Chris did today? How can you let that slide? He just snapped at his kids for no good reason. He completely lost it over nothing."

"God, did you see that TV show Chris watched last night? Not exactly G-rated entertainment."

"What about his tax return from last year? How are those tax deductions?"

"Did you see how he hid under his desk and pretended he wasn't there when that person came to see him at church?"

On and on it goes. Not that any of those hypothetical situations are true of course; I am a pastor... These are all accusations. Labels. They all speak to identity. And the enemy weaponizes each and every one of them.

Remember, if he can alter your identity, he can change your destiny.

HEAVEN'S COURTROOM

If you've ever set foot in a courtroom, you know it can be an intimidating experience. I was caught up in a bit of trouble in high school, hanging out with the wrong friends, and I wound up standing before a judge in a Manitoba courtroom. Somewhere in a sealed room at a police station, there are a handful of mug shots sitting with four smiling Christian school kids who had no idea what they were getting themselves into.

The list of charges was fairly intense: arson, possession of an accelerant, possession of an accelerant with the intent to do harm, and mischief. (By the way, I think every child on earth is guilty of that last one.)

The experience was surreal. If you're used to seeing this kind of scene on TV, it's not as much fun in person as you may have hoped. You sit quietly on one side of this huge room. There are guards at the door and people in the gallery. In hushed tones you talk to your lawyer who tries to defend you against the charges listed beside your name. He's usually overworked and underpaid.

On the other side of the expansive room is a prosecutor whose job it is to argue against you. He's literally there to accuse you. And way up there is the judge, towering over the mere mortals who've entered his hearing. The judge listens as the prosecutor lays out the charges against you, then makes his ruling.

That scene is right out of the book of Revelation. That's exactly what the enemy is up to each and every day—except that this throne room is in heaven, and the judge is God, the almighty ruler of the cosmos. Our enemy is standing there before God each day, laying out our dirty laundry and litigating our lives. What many of us don't realize is that this scene spills over into so many other parts of our story.

Those thoughts that pop into your head during the day, reminding you of all your shortcomings—those thoughts that keep playing back a highlight reel of all your mistakes—those are often not just thoughts, but accusations from the Accuser himself.

Those recurring memories of the moments you wished you could forget or the moments you would take back in a second given the chance—those aren't always just memories. They can be accusations from the enemy himself.

It's hard to overstate how important this distinction is. If you assume they're your own thoughts, you'll give them a pass. You'll think about them and consider them, or at the very least let them roll around in your head on an endless repeat. Thoughts like "I'm not good enough." Or "people don't like me." Thoughts like "You're not really a good parent; if you were you wouldn't have snapped like that." "What kind of Christian are you? Singing here on Sunday morning, hungover from the party last night. You don't belong here."

These thoughts continually bring up your past and play back your moments of weakness in a never-ending loop. Those aren't thoughts; they're accusations. And you must not take them in or assimilate them. They're labels from the enemy, and you cannot let them stick.

If you trace them back to their true source and realize who they're coming from, you'll reject them and fight back! You'll call them out as the lies they are. But early detection is everything.

WHAT GOD SEES

Early in my walk with Christ, I learned a truth I've never forgotten: *When God sees you, all he sees is Jesus.*

Think about that for a second. When God sees you, all he sees is Jesus. He doesn't see any of your mistakes, any of your sin, any of your past or your shortcomings. When God sees you, all he sees is Jesus!

Jesus's perfect righteousness.

Jesus's perfect obedience.

Jesus's white robes and unstained garments.

The biblical language David uses in Psalm 103 is "as far as the east is from the west"—that's how far God has taken our sins from us through the death of Jesus Christ. Amazing!

The life-altering reality is that we get to wear Christ's righteousness like armor on our chest each and every day—washed clean and brand new! It is armor without a single blemish or mark. God has offered us this through his Son Jesus, so no matter what the enemy's accusation is, it never sticks. Because Jesus has covered each and every part of you. What a life-altering reality! That means that nothing in your past can ever be held against you, no matter how dark or painful it was.

Let's return to that courtroom scene John described in Revelation 12, because what he described is only part of the story. If you could somehow look behind the veil and watch the rest of that scene play out, you would see one of the most amazing truths of Scripture in action. Yes, the enemy will stand before God accusing us of every mistake we've ever made. But that's not all. You would also see something breathtaking happen each and every time in response.

Every time the enemy lobs an accusation, regardless of its merit, Jesus stands up as our attorney—our advocate, the Bible says—and he objects. Each time, Jesus stands up and says, "Objection, your honor! That has already been paid for. Here's the receipt"—as he shows his nail-scarred hands and the wounds on his feet.

When the enemy regroups and tries again, cursing in his

chair, Jesus stands up and says "Objection, your honor. He's with me!" Over and over this repeats. Each time there's an accusation against us, or an indictment on our record, Jesus stands up and says, "Objection, your honor. She's with me."

Please hear me. You don't have to listen to a single one of those accusations. Not one. You don't have to allow those thoughts to haunt you, nor those memories to follow you around. You don't have to allow a single one of those labels to stick. Why? Because they're not true.

None of them.

Because of Jesus, not a single one stands. You don't have to let anyone in your life define you or dictate your future, because Jesus has bought and paid for it all. That is the solid rock on which we stand. You are not what you've done. You are not what others have spoken over you. You are who God says you are. Period.

So what do we look for? How do we keep watch? What does accusation in our lives feel like? They feel like arrows—arrows on fire.

FLAMING ARROWS

In Ephesians 6, Paul talks about the armor of God. It's one of the most amazing and descriptive passages on spiritual warfare in the Bible. And in that listing of armor he uses this powerful image of flaming arrows or fiery darts.

Shooting a bow and arrow was a big part of my life growing up. I was an archery instructor at a camp in the woods. We had a beautiful archery range set back into the forest, surrounded by trees. I can tell you from experience that a bow and arrow is a serious weapon. The sound of an arrow whistling through the air is terrifying, especially when it's haphazardly shot by inattentive teens. But Paul uses an even more graphic image—of an arrow on fire.

Historians tell us that archers used to wrap their arrows in fabric, dip them in pitch, then light them as they fired on their enemies. This intrigued me. It was an image I couldn't shake. To get a sense of what that was like, I made one myself. I've never shied away from playing with fire (that was actually how I found myself in that courtroom story I mentioned earlier), so I bought an arrow, wrapped it in a t-shirt, covered it in fuel, then lit it on fire. You should have seen the look on my son's face. All of a sudden *pastor* was a much cooler job in his eyes than it was yesterday.

If you think an arrow is scary, you've never seen one of these. I showed it to my congregation once while I was preaching, and the effect was lost on no one.

To defend themselves from the flaming arrows of the enemy, Roman soldiers used to take their wooden shields, wrap them in leather, and dip them in water before a battle. They knew what was coming. Sooner or later the sky would be filled with these incendiary darts. As the fiery darts and flaming arrows filled the sky, Roman soldiers would simply crouch and hide behind their shields. All you had to do was wait. Your only job was to stand behind your shield and listen for the *tsssss* sound of the fire being extinguished.

When faced with the fiery darts of accusation, our response should be exactly the same. We must stand behind the shield of faith and let it extinguish the arrows of the evil one. "Take up the shield of faith, with which you can extinguish all the flaming arrows of the evil one" (Ephesians 6:16).

When the enemy says that you're just a nobody, remind

yourself: "No, I am loved and chosen, and I have royal blood flowing through my veins! I am a son or daughter of the King!" (1 Peter 2:9).

When he reminds you of your darkest moments and biggest mistakes, reply that you're a "new creation in Christ" (2 Corinthians 5:17). What's past is gone, and you're brand new!

When he says, "Nobody really cares about you," remind yourself: "Jesus cares! Enough to die for me" (John 3:16).

When the enemy tells you that you have no future, tell him you'll one day sit on a throne and rule with Christ (2 Timothy 2:12)—and that he should be careful, because one day you'll crush him beneath your feet (Romans 16:20)!

Every accusation has a corresponding truth in Scripture to counteract it—a truth about who you really are in Christ Jesus. And that's exactly how we extinguish the flaming arrows of the evil one.

Faith.

The shield of faith.

Faith in who God says you are—not who the enemy or anyone else tries to convince you that you've been. God's truths must replace those lies and labels we've been listening to.

The list below has been a life saver for me through the years of my faith journey. I read it first when I was sixteen, and I've gone back to it again and again. Read it and remember. Memorize the lines that deal with your weakest areas. It will have a profound effect on your identity.

Who You Are in Christ

Because you are in Christ, every one of these statements is true of you:

- I am loved. (1 John 3:3)
- I am accepted. (Ephesians 1:6)
- I am a child of God. (John 1:12)

- I am Jesus's friend. (John 15:14)
- I am a joint heir with Jesus, sharing his inheritance with him. (Romans 8:17)
- I am united with God and one spirit with him. (1 Corinthians 6:17)
- I am a temple of God; his Spirit lives in me. (1 Corinthians 6:19)
- I am a member of Christ's body. (1 Corinthians 12:27)
- I am a saint. (Ephesians 1:1)
- I am redeemed and forgiven. (Colossians 1:14)
- I am complete in Jesus Christ. (Colossians 2:10)
- I am free from condemnation. (Romans 8:1)
- I am a new creation. (2 Corinthians 5:17)
- I am chosen by God, holy and dearly loved. (Colossians 3:12)
- I am established, anointed, and sealed by God. (2 Corinthians 1:21)
- I do not have a spirit of fear, but of love, power, and a sound mind. (2 Timothy 1:7)
- I am God's co-worker. (2 Corinthians 6:1)
- I am seated in heavenly places with Christ. (Ephesians 2:6)
- I have direct access to God. (Ephesians. 2:18)
- I am chosen to bear fruit. (John 15:16)
- I am one of God's living stones, being built up in Christ as a spiritual house. (1 Peter 2:5)
- God will never leave me. (Hebrews 13:5)
- God works in me to help me do the things he wants me to do. (Philippians 2:13)
- I can ask God for wisdom, and he'll give me exactly what I need (James 1:5).

8

The Lie of:
Discouragement

Things Will Never Change

Therefore, if anyone is in Christ,
he is a new creation; the old has gone,
the new has come!
2 CORINTHIANS 5:17

Years ago I attended a pastors' conference where the keynote speaker was H. B. London. A decade later, I still remember the message he preached on Saturday night. That in and of itself is kind of a miracle. Most of us have trouble remembering what the pastor preached the next day, let alone ten years ago.

London's message had a catchy title—"Joy Suckers"—and it began with a story. He was pastoring a church in America's Midwest, and they had two morning services, at nine and eleven. One Sunday morning, he seemed particularly on fire as he preached at the nine o'clock service. He considered it one of the best messages he'd preached in his life. The people were responsive, and the presence of God was overwhelming. It's hard to describe for someone who has never preached, but for a pastor, there's no greater feeling on earth than to see God show up like this. London walked out of that service with a smile on his face a mile wide.

Between the two services he went to grab something from his office, and as he was walking through the courtyard back to the sanctuary, he was approached by Gladys, an older lady in the church. She caught him and said, "Pastor, do you have a second?" When a conversation begins with those six words, there's no telling what direction it's headed. Somehow he knew he shouldn't stay and talk, but he was trapped. He paused to listen to Gladys, and she started in on him.

First, it was about the earlier service that morning, then it was about the church as a whole. She criticized nearly everything he was involved in, including some things he had absolutely no control over. After a few minutes, when she was finished, he said he felt like crawling away. When the assault was over, he felt no more than three inches tall. Somehow in that brief conversation, she managed to suck the life right out of him after one of the greatest mornings of his life.

That's often how it goes, isn't it? It's almost like some people are on assignment. When he thought back on that morning, the only way he could explain it was to say it was almost like she walked up to him, fastened a small hose to his heart, and sucked the joy right out.

When he preached later at the eleven o'clock service, the fire had gone out. His sermon was D.O.A. The room seemed lifeless. People were yawning, fiddling with the candy in their pockets, wondering where they were going for lunch.

Ministry is *heart* work—and at that moment, his heart was empty.

He came up with the name Joy Suckers for these kinds of people in our lives. I bet you've met one or two of them before— the kind of people who can suck the life right out of you in a matter of minutes.

In her defense, I don't think Gladys had any idea what she was doing, or that she'd caused the death of a sermon in four minutes flat. But H. B. London's story stuck with me—because I've lived through a version of it dozens of times. It's an illustration of just how powerful discouragement can be when it roots down into our lives, and how quickly it can rob us of any kind of heart. The truth is, it's not just people that can be Joy Suckers; sometimes situations are so hard that our hearts become an empty shell. Which is why we're told in Proverbs, "Above all else, guard your heart, for everything you do flows from it" (Proverbs 4:23). The *English Standard Version* translates that verse this way: "Keep your heart with all vigilance, for from it flow the springs of life." This has been a key verse for me at various times in my walk with Christ. If you've ever struggled with not just discouragement, but its deeper relatives—despair and depression—you know how true this verse can be. When your heart is wounded, everything else in life is affected, because everything you do flows from it. It's like someone took the batteries right out of your chest, and it's all you can do just to get out of bed.

THE MIRACLE AND MAYHEM ON MOUNT CARMEL

Discouragement is a familiar foe for many of us. In fact, I don't know a single person who's immune to it. I would say that of all the lies I wrestle with, discouragement is among the one or two I struggle with most.

Discouragement has many faces. Sometimes the lie will say, "You're all alone." It will convince you that everyone has abandoned you, and no one is at your side.

Perhaps in a season of singleness it will tell you, "You'll never meet someone. This is it."

Or in challenging times, it may sound like this: "Nothing good will ever come of this. Everything you've done has been meaningless."

Ultimately, here's the lie underneath them all: "Things will never change. It's hopeless." It will whisper to you at the bottom of a valley: "This is all there is, and you're stuck here forever."

Truthfully, an idea like this doesn't seem all that dangerous. I mean, how bad can a little discouragement be? But that's the thing—it's never just a little bit. When it rains, it pours. And when we fall into the depths of that valley, it can take every ounce of energy we have just to make breakfast.

Just ask Elijah.

In 1 Kings 18, Elijah performed one of the greatest miracles in the entire Old Testament. It became legendary. Little Jewish children would reenact it on the playground for centuries to come. He defeated and completely embarrassed the 450 prophets of Baal that the evil King Ahab had gathered on top of Mount Carmel. Elijah did this in style—he called down fire from heaven to prove once and for all that Yahweh is the one true God, and that Baal was only an impostor. It was a literal lightning bolt hurled from the heavens at his request. Elijah even taunted the prophets of Baal as they cried out uselessly to a fake god who wasn't listening. Then he prayed for rain, and a cloud began to gather in the sky after years of drought.

Elijah was a spiritual giant.

I've stood on Mount Carmel where all this took place, and it's breathtaking—not just the view, but the realization of what actually happened there. I brought home a rock from the peak just to remind myself of this title fight. This was one of the greatest victories in the entire Old Testament. But then, in the next chapter of 1 Kings, we encounter Jezebel, chief of the Joy Suckers:

> Now Ahab told Jezebel everything Elijah had done and how he had killed all the prophets with the sword. So Jezebel sent a messenger to Elijah to say, "May the gods deal with me, be it ever so severely, if by this time tomorrow I do not make your life like that of one of them."
>
> Elijah was afraid and ran for his life. When he came to Beersheba in Judah, he left his servant there, while he

himself went a day's journey into the wilderness. He came to a broom bush, sat down under it and prayed that he might die. "I have had enough, Lord," he said. "Take my life; I am no better than my ancestors." Then he lay down under the bush and fell asleep.

All at once an angel touched him and said, "Get up and eat." He looked around, and there by his head was some bread baked over hot coals, and a jar of water. He ate and drank and then lay down again.

The angel of the Lord came back a second time and touched him and said, "Get up and eat, for the journey is too much for you." So he got up and ate and drank. Strengthened by that food, he traveled forty days and forty nights until he reached Horeb, the mountain of God. There he went into a cave and spent the night. (1 Kings 19:1-9)

After Jezebel threatened to kill him Elijah ran as far south as he possibly could, found a broom tree (more like a bush), and asked God to take his life. He'd had enough. He said, "God, my life is over, my ministry is useless, I'm no better than my ancestors."

Elijah was done. He was down and out. At first you might think he was just afraid of Jezebel, but listen closely to his words; this isn't fear, it's despair. He was convinced that his ministry was a failure, and he just couldn't continue on. If you've ever felt the crushing weight of discouragement, then you at least know a little of the battle Elijah was fighting.

Was he a failure? Were his feelings accurate? Had his entire ministry been a waste? Not on your life. He'd just experienced one of the most stunning victories in biblical history—complete with fire from heaven! I'd call that a pretty big win. If I could pull that off, my inbox would be full of job offers. Today, three thousand years later, there's a statue of Elijah on Mount Carmel commemorating his spectacular triumph.

The Lie of: **Discouragement**

And that was only twenty-four hours before this passage we read—the day before discouragement ambushed him and left him for dead. But feelings don't always make sense, do they? Sometimes discouragement is irrational. You can hear ten compliments and one criticism, and you stew on the one detractor all night.

After I preach a message on Sunday, I can hear ten great responses about my message along with one veiled dig, and guess which one I'm thinking about when my head hits the pillow? I can't tell you how often this story plays out. Why in the world do we listen to the one instead of the ten? Why do we fixate on the negative voices in our head? Because discouragement is a powerful thing. In fact, psychologists say that this ten-to-one ratio is about right—it takes eleven compliments to offset one criticism. Our minds require eleven words of affirmation to undo one word of attack. Sometimes all the logic in the world is no match for an emotional tidal wave like this.

EAT, SLEEP, REPEAT

So what does God do when his prophet is lying in a heap, ready to quit? What is his redemptive plan?

Here's the fascinating answer: God feeds him, and gets him to sleep, then repeats this sequence all over again.

It's easy to want to pass this by, but that would be a tragic mistake. This isn't mere filler—the Bible doesn't contain any. Elijah comes to God with what presents like a spiritual problem, and God responds first with a physical solution. This may seem insignificant, but it's a profound piece of wisdom.

If you're struggling with discouragement right now, let me ask you a few questions:

How's your diet?

How's your sleep schedule?

When was the last time you truly rested?

See, in the story of Elijah, each of the lanes intersect. We are physical beings as well as spiritual beings. We're composed of body, mind, and spirit, and discouragement functions on all three levels. It reaches into the physical, mental, and spiritual dimensions of our lives. In our struggle with discouragement and depression, the results of our efforts are often deeply underwhelming, because the prescription addresses only one or two of these contributing factors.

Here with Elijah, God's tailored solution addresses all three dimensions in a truly holistic sense. And God begins with food and rest.

H.I.T.

A pastor I grew up listening to used to say this all the time: Satan loves to HIT you when you're *H*ungry, *I*solated, *T*ired.

I've never forgotten it. I write here as much from exegesis as experience. You and I are most vulnerable when we're hungry, isolated, or tired. The enemy knows when we're weak:

- when you're hungry for food, or companionship, or any other God-given need that's currently going unmet;
- when you're isolated and alone, without a community to encourage you and hold you up;
- when you're tired—physically, emotionally, or mentally.

It's like walking through the grocery store when you're starving. Or surfing the internet when you're lonely or exhausted. We tend to make remarkably poor choices when we're in a state of depletion.

A study was done on Israeli justices who were in charge of parole applications from prison inmates. It was a fascinating experiment. They looked at what time of day the judges ate, and compared this with whether or not they granted parole for the applicant. It sounds ridiculous, but they found that right after eating a meal, the judges granted nearly 65 percent of applications, compared with the overall average of 35 percent. Even more troubling was the finding that ten minutes before a meal, when hunger was at its peak, the approval rate for parole requests was near zero. That's a scary thought. After lunch, banishing hunger from the equation, the numbers improved remarkably, only to plummet just before quitting time. It turned out that getting your parole request granted had more to do with how many cheerios your judge ate than the merits of your case.[10] After reading this, I vowed never to make a big decision on an empty stomach.

None of these things like hunger, isolation, and exhaustion are wrong in and of themselves, but they each leave us vulnerable to temptation and the lies of the enemy.

Jesus experienced all three of these conditions when he met Satan in the wilderness. In Luke's narrative of Jesus's encounter, he ends with a curious phrase. After the devil had been defeated, Luke tells us that he left Jesus "until an opportune time" (Luke 4:13). Think about the implications of those words. You and I are clearly more vulnerable at some times than at others. There are "opportune times" for him to attack us. It would seem we have windows of weakness. What are yours? Have you ever thought about them?

These kinds of weaknesses often follow a mountaintop experience. Have you ever returned from an amazing weekend of spiritual growth and found a hurricane waiting for you at home? That Monday morning can be traumatizing. Pastors often report Sunday afternoon as their weakest point of the week. They find that temptation is most appealing right after they've just spent Sunday morning doing the work of the kingdom.

Both Elijah and Jesus had just come off a spiritual mountaintop—Elijah's literal mountaintop victory, and Jesus's public baptism, when the Spirit descended on him like a dove.

As counterintuitive as it sounds, we must be especially vigilant after victory. That's when the enemy is often waiting with an ambush.

When we're feeling the weight of discouragement, we need to check our vitals. We need to make sure our hunger and exhaustion aren't causing our despair. Duffy Robbins used to say, "Sometimes the most spiritual thing you can do is something unspiritual."[11] I know that sounds funny, maybe even a tad heretical, but it's true. By unspiritual, he didn't mean sinful, but rather physical, relational, or emotional.

Just as God saw with Elijah, sometimes the roots of our struggle reach far into the areas you least expect. In many of these valleys, sleep, food, and a little exercise or real relationship might do you wonders. I can tell you as a pastor that a good vacation has cured the majority of my discouragement nine times out of ten.

God's first prescription is: Eat, sleep, repeat.

REACH OUT

The next thing God does with Elijah is to ask him a question. "What are you doing here, Elijah?"

You may have heard this before, and it's true: When God asks a question, he's not searching for information. When God asks a question, it's for *you*, not for him. God already knows the answer. As an omnipotent (all powerful) and omniscient (all knowing) God, there is nothing hidden from his sight, yet he asks questions throughout the Bible.

Whenever these questions arrive for us, we need to realize they have a purpose. Here in 1 Kings 19, God wanted Elijah to fully express what he was dealing with. God wanted him to put words to the cauldron of emotions bubbling inside. God was after brutal unfiltered honesty.

When it comes to our negative emotions, many of us were taught to hold them back, hold them in. Either we've been explicitly taught that, or implicitly trained by the people in our lives to bottle up negative emotions (*Nobody wants to hear those,* we think, *especially not God*). Sometimes we assume that somehow they're a sign of a lack of faith. But with Elijah, God himself proves us all wrong. He actually draws out these negative thoughts from Elijah.

Remember this: If God didn't want to hear it, he never would have asked in the first place.

Overall, as Christians, we still don't seem to know what to do with our emotions. Many Christians are spiritual giants and emotional infants. It's a sad juxtaposition. The Bible expresses the full spectrum of human emotion and encourages us to bring them all to God in whatever state we find ourselves.

I've often said that when it comes to feelings, we should be *honest* about our emotions and *faithful* in what we do with them. That's the most biblical way to think about our feelings, as far as I can tell. If you ignore them, they'll swell up with a terrifying strength, then one day break the dam and destroy just about everything you know. But if you obey them, they'll get you into just about as much trouble.

The biblical prescription is to be honest about our emotions, and faithful with what we do with them.

God can handle our deepest and darkest emotions. He's big enough for that. We don't need to sanitize our prayers on God's account. Just listen to the ranting and raving of David in the Psalms, or to Job in the book that bears his name. In my early years as a Christian these were the books of the Bible that saved my life. When I was drowning in frustration and emotion, I took Job's example as a template to follow, and it was a lifeline. I brought to God everything I was feeling, no matter how fierce or ugly. After I'd spent every last ounce of my anger and my pain, he was waiting there for me with his arms open wide.

God can handle our discouragement and our anger as well as our outbursts of frustration. Sometimes we try to hide our darkest feelings from God, but in the end it's the worst thing we can do. We need to get those emotions out, not stuff them farther in.

As he was dealing with Elijah, God needed to interrupt the internal monologue of dark thoughts in Elijah's head and get him talking. If you're anything like me, you know how dangerous it can be to get stuck in your own head. You know how wild the funhouse can get when there's no one else there to talk some sense into you. As Tony Evans says, "*You* talking to *you* isn't always a healthy thing." In fact, you talking to you can be a dangerous thing. You talking to you rarely solves anything, unless you're speaking truth to madness. Otherwise, it becomes a downward thought spiral. It transforms into an echo chamber that amplifies each time it comes back around. It can lead to some pretty dark places if all you're doing is letting your own thoughts run wild.

That's exactly what has happened to Elijah. The enemy got into his head, and discouragement found its way into his heart. Satan planted some lies in his ear, then spun the top and walked away. He whispered that Elijah's life was over, that his work was useless, that he was all alone. He told him that Jezebel would have his head by the end of the week. They were all lies, every last one of them, but Elijah was too weak to reject them.

Sometimes you need someone else with you to break that spiral. You need a friend or God himself to speak truth and break the cycle.

I nearly made the biggest mistake of my life when I was stuck in my own head. My relationship with my wife was almost over before it began, and it still scares me when I think about it. After we'd just started dating, I nearly ended things because I didn't think it was going to work. I barely even remember why. I didn't tell this to anyone; I'd just convinced myself it was true.

84

The Lie of: **Discouragement**

About an hour before I planned to break off the relationship, I told my friend Lyndon what I was going to do.

He looked at me and said, "You're an idiot." He just kept saying it over and over—it's burned in my memory. "You're an idiot"—for letting a girl like that go, he would say. He shook his head slowly and ominously as he said it, never taking his eyes off me.

Turns out, he was right. I was being an idiot. I just couldn't see it. Lyndon actually rescued me from the brink of an all-out train wreck that may have changed the course of my life.

Sometimes being inside your head is a scary place to be for too long, and that goes for discouragement too. So reach out—to God and to someone else. You need to stop talking to yourself and let someone else break the spiral. In this fight, prayer and community are everything.

TWENTY/TWENTY VISION

The last thing God did for Elijah was to reorient him by clarifying what he was seeing.

The ultimate danger of discouragement is that it warps your vision. When you're discouraged, it's not just one thing that's wrong—everything's wrong! Right? It's not just one person who's mad at you; it feels like everyone's mad at you. Everything becomes exaggerated, pervasive, and permanent. Instead of thinking, "Man, this is hard right now," the thought becomes, "Things are never going to change! I'll never get out of this!" That lie slowly works its way into everything you see and every word you hear.

Discouragement robs you of perspective and leaves you with two things in its place: tunnel vision and amnesia.

Tunnel vision is a type of hyper-focus. In this case, all you can see is the problem, and nothing else is clear. The more you stare at your situation, the larger it grows in your mind and heart. If you constantly stare at the problem, it grows to the size of a mountain that seems too large to climb.

Amnesia is the inability to remember. When it comes to discouragement, you can't seem to remember anything other than the problem at hand—including all the other times God has rescued you and provided for you.

Case in point: Elijah couldn't even remember twenty-four hours ago when fire fell from heaven and rain clouds began to fill the sky at his request. This is why the word *remember* is so dominant in the book of Deuteronomy—because we're prone to spiritual amnesia.

Elijah said, "I'm the last one left! There's no one else." But God answered, "No, Elijah, there are seven thousand others who have not bowed to Baal." Elijah was *not* the last one left. Not by any count. Besides those seven thousand God mentioned, there were also a hundred prophets of Yahweh stashed away in two different caves still loyal to God. But the enemy had whispered in Elijah's ear: "It's all over. Nothing you've done matters. You're the last one standing, and you're all alone."

Perhaps you recognize those thoughts. Maybe you're hearing them right now. They're lies, but Elijah was unable to spot them. The adversary disguised them as his thoughts, just like he does with you and me. And Elijah allowed them entry into his soul.

God gave his prophet a new perspective. His final act was a reorientation of sorts. He gave Elijah a new set of glasses through which to see the world. When he split the rocks with a tornado, shook the mountain with an earthquake, and burned in the inferno, God's unmatched power was on display. But then, God truly revealed himself in a whisper—the still small voice.

That's what we need to listen for: the truth. The truth that can rescue us from the pit that despair has thrown us in.

And here's the truth: *You are not alone. Your work is never useless. God will never leave nor forsake you.*

Whatever storm clouds are gathering in your life, this too shall pass, and there's a bright future ahead of you. These are all absolute promises in Scripture. Jezebel has no authority over you! She's been lying to you, and it's time you stopped listening.

GUARD YOUR HEART

Watch out for Joy Suckers—in person and in thought. Watch out for the overwhelming torrent of emotions that drags you further and further down.

You can't always avoid them. Sometimes they'll corner you. But you don't have to listen.

Remember the words of Solomon, the ever wise king: "Above all else, guard your heart, for everything you do flows from it." Hold on to that verse, even in the darkest night.

I've been in ministry for almost two decades now. I started young—really young. And I almost didn't make it past my second year. I was twenty-two, working in a church where I knew no one. I was an associate pastor fifteen hundred miles from home. My wife and I began this brave new adventure in another part of the country, and those two years were intense. Actually, the word *intense* doesn't even begin to describe it. We didn't know it then, but we'd parachuted into a church that was just about to split. It turned out to be an unmitigated disaster. The senior pastor I worked for said it was the worst scenario he'd ever seen, and he'd been leading churches for thirty-five years.

Those two years ended up with a long list of resignations. The senior pastor resigned, then the other associate, and I was the last to go. God had released us. Those first twenty-four months of ministry turned out to be baptism by fire, and we went all the way back home to bind our wounds and mend our hearts.

To say I was discouraged doesn't even begin to touch the level of darkness I felt. Here I was living back at home with my family until we could decipher what came next.

Slowly and quietly that summer, I started to feel the call to go back—back to the place where things had burned. A few hundred of the people I'd led at the church and who had split wanted me to come back and start a church plant. The thought alone was terrifying, and the day before we left, the two closest people in my life tried to talk me out of it.

My dad pulled me aside and took me into a back room. He hadn't done that since I was seven. He said, "Listen, son. I know you feel called back, but why don't you just stay? You know how hard the last two years were. You don't need to do this."

Three hours later, my best friend repeated those words nearly verbatim. It was almost like they'd planned this. There was an orchestration to it. My friend said, "I know you feel God calling you back, but just stay here. Maybe something else will come up. We're all here—why don't you just stay?"

Coming into those conversations with the depth of despair I'd felt earlier that year was almost too much—almost more than I could bear. But I realized in that moment that the still small voice inside me was saying something else, and these other voices had an uncomfortable ring to them.

The next day I left. I ran. I ran toward where God was calling, and I've never looked back. Since then, we've seen God do amazing things in the churches he has called us to, and that former season feels like an eternity ago. In the moment, I was sure things would never change, and that all the seeds God had planted would lie dormant forever. But that season did pass, and those seeds sprouted in the monsoon. I was sure that was the end, but it was anything but. God brought good out of the most painful season of my life—just as he will with yours! In fact, that's exactly what he promises: "We know that in all things God works for the good of those who love him, who have been called according to his purpose" (Romans 8:28).

Be encouraged. Despair is never the end of the story. Sometimes, it's just the beginning.

9

The Lie of: Distraction

It Doesn't Matter What You Do with Your Time and Attention

"Martha, Martha," the Lord answered,
"you are worried and upset about many things,
but few things are needed—or indeed only one.
Mary has chosen what is better,
and it will not be taken away from her."
LUKE 10:41-42

I don't know if you've noticed lately, but we live in an incredibly distracted society. It's not just that we occasionally lose our train of thought, or forget something important, but that distraction has become a way of life, the very air we breathe.

We do with it what we do with everything we're not proud of—we call it something else. We're not distracted; we're simply multitasking. Right? Somehow we've made a virtue out of a liability.

I can't tell you how many times I've vowed to spend less time on my phone and more with my wife and kids, only to be glued to it again a week later. I'm sure I'm not the only one. I remember seeing my five-year-old grab a calculator one day and furiously start pounding the digits. I asked him what he was doing, and he said, "Just texting, Dad!" I wasn't sure if I should laugh or cry.

I don't think any of us willfully chose to live like this. It just kind of happened. Life started coming at us faster and faster each day, and it felt like our only choice was to sink or swim. But it's not without side effects. The byproducts of a frenetic life are the twin dangers of a noisy world and a noisy heart, and we wrestle with them every single day.

The *Huffington Post* ran an article a few years ago that drove this home for me. It began with a picture, one that could have been from any mass transit anywhere around the world. It was a run-of-the-mill Monday morning commute, with a handful of strangers standing and sitting on the bus en route to wherever their day was taking them. Every single person had their heads buried deep into the alternate reality of their smartphones, completely unaware of anything happening around them.[12]

Now, unfortunately that scene is nothing special. We see it every day in line at the grocery store, or sitting at an airport waiting for a flight. Sad, but nothing new. But, it wasn't the picture that was startling, it's what happened off camera right beside it.

On this particular bus ride there was a man who pulled out a gun. Right there in broad daylight, he produced a handgun out of his jacket pocket and displayed it for all to see. In reality, most morning commutes are a fairly sleepy affair, but I would imagine coffee would be redundant on a morning like that. As everyone was minding their own business, all of a sudden here was a catalyst for mass panic.

Here's the crazy thing—one I could barely believe as I read it:

Nobody noticed.

Nobody.

Not one person on that bus was even aware a man had taken a gun out of his jacket. Then, almost as if to prove a point, he did it again, then again. Three times he brandished a firearm on a packed bus full of people, yet there were no screams, no pandemonium. No one rushed toward the door. Incredibly, not one person even looked up.

Sometimes reality is stranger than fiction.

Not too long after this story, a California newspaper published an article about a woman who'd fallen off a cliff. She hadn't been pushed, or accidentally slipped; she simply walked right off the edge while texting. Yes, you read that right. She was messaging a friend, and was so absorbed in their conversation she stopped looking where she was going and fell two hundred feet headlong onto the rugged shoreline. After thirteen hours at the bottom of a Palos Verdes cliff, her cries for help were overheard by a passing hiker, who promptly dialed 911. The police showed up with a helicopter and had to airlift her off the rocky beach.

When I think about the world we're living in, I often think of those two stories. They're burned into my memory. You'll never see these two images on the next iPhone commercial—it doesn't fit the narrative they're selling—but these are the unintended consequences of a world that's no longer paying attention. These are stories from the dark side of distraction.

This chronic inability to focus or be present in the everyday moments of our lives isn't just a nuisance anymore; it has become an epidemic. It's slowly but surely stealing from us the most important things in our lives. We carry around these weapons of mass distraction in our pocket everywhere we go, and if the scientists are right, they're literally rewiring our brains, our relationships, even our hearts.

As I watch the throngs of people in public staring at their phones, there are times when I'm convinced the zombie apocalypse has begun, and no one's doing a thing about it.

There's a lie we've come to believe in this information age that doesn't seem all that dangerous at first. It's the lie that what we do with our time and attention doesn't matter. As long as we give God his one hour on Sunday, we can do whatever we want with the rest.

But this lie is nowhere near as innocent as it seems. Those hours in front of our colorful little rectangles are forming and shaping us from the inside out, one pixel at a time. In fact, it has become a powerful tool in the hands of our enemy.

It turns out that distraction can keep us from God's plan for our lives—not by flashy sin, but by inattentive sloth.

Whether or not you realize it, there's a connection between the way we spend our time and the destination we arrive at. There's a connection between what we focus on and who we grow into. And it's even more powerful than that. *Our attention actually determines our direction in life*—and what you stare at profoundly influences who you become.

Listen to John Mark Comer:

> What you give your attention to is the person you become. Put another way: the mind is the portal to the soul, and what you fill your mind with will shape the trajectory of your character. In the end, your life is no more than the sum of what you gave your attention to. That bodes well for those apprentices of Jesus who give the bulk of their attention to him and to all that is good, beautiful, and true in his world. But not for those who give their attention to the 24/7 news cycle of outrage and anxiety and emotion-charged drama, or to the nonstop feed of celebrity gossip, titillation, and cultural drivel. (As if we "give" it in the first place; much of it is stolen by a clever algorithm out to monetize our precious attention.) But again: we become what we give our attention to, for better or worse.[13]

The shocking truth that many of us are unaware of is this: *Attention determines direction.* This is one of the immutable laws of development. Our inputs determine our outputs.

In determining the course of our physical and spiritual lives, time and attention are the two precious commodities. So what are we doing with ours? That's the question we need to start asking.

SEED AND GROUND

One of my favorite parables of Jesus is the one about the sower. It's deceptively simple and easy to overlook.

A farmer goes out to scatter his seed, as he intends to plant a crop. First he scatters his seed on the hard path, but birds come and eat it up. Next he scatters on the rocky soil, but despite a quick start, they die from the curse of shallow roots. On another plot he scatters seed on good ground riddled with weeds. This time the seeds shoot up, but so do the weeds, and in the end the weeds choke the good seed out. Finally the farmer scatters his seed on good soil, and it's a bumper crop. It produces a thirty-fold, sixtyfold, or hundredfold return on his investment.

Rarely does Jesus explain his parables. Often we're left to scratch our heads and seek his heart. The power of a parable is in the way it forces us to wrestle with the story long before we comprehend it. It's almost as if they're Trojan horses filled with truth, able to sneak past our defenses and unpack. But this time, for whatever reason, here Jesus pulls back the curtain and gives his explanation:

> Listen then to what the parable of the sower means: When anyone hears the message about the kingdom and does not understand it, the evil one comes and snatches away what was sown in their heart. This is the seed sown along the path. The seed falling on rocky ground refers to someone who hears the word and at once receives it with joy. But since they have no root, they last only a short time. When trouble or persecution comes because of the word, they quickly fall away. The seed falling among the thorns refers to someone who hears the word, but the worries of this life and the deceitfulness of wealth

choke the word, making it unfruitful. But the seed falling on good soil refers to someone who hears the word and understands it. This is the one who produces a crop, yielding a hundred, sixty, or thirty times what was sown. (Matthew 13:18-23)

According to Jesus, God is the farmer, the seed is his word, and the ground is our hearts. So far so good. And it's easy to look around and see this story playing out every single day in the lives of our friends and family. It's easy to see this truth in everyone else. But that's the easy way out. The parables of Jesus were meant not so you and I could elbow the person sitting next to us, but to make us search our own hearts, our own souls—to see who we are.

So let's ask the question Jesus wants us to: What kind of soil are we inside?

Are we hard and resistant—like the beaten path? Too closed off and armored up to hear what God is saying to us and to let it in? Have we allowed lean years and painful storms to pack down hard the soil of our souls, to the point that nothing can break through?

Are we shallow and short-sighted? Are we present while the going is good, but gone when it gets hard? Do we wither away when the heat turns up? Do we lack the root system and depth we need to survive a drought?

Are we good soil where seeds sprout fast and furious, but so do all the weeds around us? Are we surrounded by competing needs and desires, never sure which one will win out?

Or are we the deep and rich black earth that's ready for what God is doing in our lives, and willing to see it multiply? Are we ready for the harvest?

It's a hard question—because I didn't ask what you *want* to be, but which one best describes your heart. It's easy to pick the Sunday school answer. But which one hits closer to the mark?

The deeper I've stared into this parable, the more I see myself in the third kind of earth. At this stage of my walk with Christ, I often feel like the fertile ground covered in weeds—with precious little real estate available for God to grow what he wants to grow in my life.

The picture is rather profound. If you've tended a garden or a lawn, you know exactly what it means. The first summer after we moved into our current house, we planted a garden, having never had the space for one before. Back in our first home, the yard was covered by century-old maples forming an impenetrable canopy that only the slightest amount of light could pass through. When we moved, we vowed that our new place would be different. My wife was on a mission—apparently to grow everything known to man in forty square feet. We made the rookie mistake of planting everything far too close together, and it was an absolute jungle as the summer progressed. Our cat used to emerge from it like a predator from the Amazon.

Though the crowded garden was a problem, we made one even larger mistake: zucchini. That was it. I love zucchini, usually when it's in some type of cake, but if you've ever grown it, you know what I'm talking about. We planted four of them—all close together. I don't know why the lady at the garden center didn't warn us, but they took over the place. Each of them grew to four feet tall and six feet across and they produced zucchini at a rate I've never seen equaled. We harvested it every day and couldn't keep up.

After we ate zucchini for breakfast, lunch, and dinner, and baked it into everything we possibly could, we were still drowning in it. We had zucchini in the freezer for two solid years. (I recently found an old bag of it in the basement deep freeze). To this day, I still have nightmares about it.

I tell you all this because it illustrates an element of Jesus's parable. You and I are finite creatures. We're limited human beings. We have only so much space in our hearts. We have only so much time, energy, and attention, and there's only so much real estate to work with. You can have zucchini, or you can have a garden—but not both.

Here's the underlying truth: If we're not careful, other things in our lives will crowd out what God is actively growing in us, and will choke out the seeds of life.

WORRY, WEEDS, AND WEALTH

Jesus mentions the twin weeds of worry and wealth, but I believe these were just two examples of a multitude of things that can function like thorns in our souls. They were placeholders of sorts. This wasn't an exhaustive list, but simply something to get us started. There are a number of distracting weeds that will grow fast and furious alongside the good seed God is sowing in us. If we're not careful, those things will choke the life right out of what God is doing in us. The weeds are competing for the same time, energy, and attention we need to divert to our spiritual life and growth, but often those resources go to the noisy color boxes in our pockets and on our nightstands before we zonk out.

For many of us, if we're honest, there isn't room in our hearts for God to speak to us because we spend every second of the day buried in distraction. I increasingly find myself in this camp. There isn't room to pray and talk to God because we're so scatterbrained we can't focus for long enough. We can't think about the timeless truths of Scripture or the theological building blocks of our faith because we never seem to be able to focus and dig deep enough.

In fact, these days it's hard to think deeply about *anything*—because we think a little bit about everything. Our minds are like skipping stones skimming the water's surface—always moving, never actually sinking in.

As a pastor, I worry about social media apps that cycle through videos every fifteen seconds. It's not just the content on the screens; I wonder how a teenager who's used to something new every fifteen seconds is ever going to listen to me preach for half an hour. That used to be a small amount of time, but in today's pace it's an eternity.

Distraction—it seems so innocent, until you realize how it works. Instead of chasing the God-ordained future he has written for us, we while away our time on Candy Crush and researching the painting techniques of Middle Eastern art.

THE SIREN'S SONG

Mass media isn't the only path to distraction. There are a thousand other adventures in missing the point. Sometimes it's the good things that are suffocating your soul. Ironically, it can even be the God things in your life—filling your schedule so much "serving" that you never actually spend time with him. The weeds come in endless varieties, but the little rectangles we carry around with us have turned distraction into a way of life.

I recently learned that the average person checks their phone every four minutes, every waking hour of the day. (You have probably checked your phone a number of times already while reading this book.) If you do the math, the picture's more than a little frightening. Checking every four minutes adds up to 240 times each and every day. Those 240 interactions add up to 4.8 hours before the clock resets, and a total of 33 hours each and every week.[14] And remember, this is just for your phone, and doesn't include time on a tablet or watching TV.

We spend more than one in seven days every week on our phone. Let it run for an average lifetime, and that's sixteen years of your life. On Candy Crush. Think about that.

Teenagers are the allstars in this competition. Take all those numbers and almost double them if you're between the ages of thirteen and eighteen. If the pattern holds, that will add up to more than twenty years of your life.[15]

Remember, we're finite creatures. Time, energy, and attention come in limited quantities. We'll invest them somewhere. What if the weeds in our lives have siphoned off the life-giving water and nutrients God meant for our souls?

THREE LIFELINES

So what do we do? How do we fight back? Should we all get together, walk down to the river, and toss in our phones? Maybe. I've seriously considered it. But the more I think about it, the more I'm convinced it won't last. I would wager we would all see each other in line at Best Buy two weeks later, staring at the ground trying to avoid eye contact.

Should we all become Luddites? Luddites were fanatics in England during the Industrial Revolution, and they used to sneak into factories at night and smash all the technology they could get their hands on. They would destroy as many machines as they could. Should we have phone-smashing parties? Perhaps. But I still think the win would be short-lived.

We could all trade our smart phones in for dumb phones. It's possible to live like that—but it won't solve all our problems, because distraction comes in too many forms.

One clever man who was committed to this fight even invented a helmet to help him focus. He called it the Isolator.

Frustrated by all the hours he wasted in ridiculous pursuits, Hugo Gernsback invented this device to block them all. It was lined with cork and covered in felt, and had a steady flow of oxygen pumped in for good measure. As impressive as that is, he found that there were just as many distractions waiting inside his own head as there were on the outside.[16]

Distraction is a many-headed beast. It's our modern day Hydra, with countless manifestations. We need a solution that transcends them all.

To win this battle, we must start by confronting the lie we've come to believe, because it *does* matter what we do with our time and attention. Attention determines direction, and it will affect the trajectory of our lives.

Sometimes our inability to focus is dependent not just on what we're doing right now, but on what we've been doing all week. Once we're willing to admit that, there are several ways we can fight back. We can refocus ourselves with the spiritual disciplines that God teaches us in his Word. They're lifelines for the weary soul. They're practices that Christians have been observing for centuries, habits that have rescued them from the man-eating plants that invade the gardens of our hearts.

Here they are: *Silence. Solitude. Fasting.*

This rhythm has persisted for millennia. Christians have been practicing them for thousands of years, and they've become the building blocks of a faithful follower of Jesus for every bit as long.

SILENCE

Silence is exactly what it sounds like—simply being quiet for a period of time. For those who've never tried it, this can be terrifying at first. We're so accustomed to noise that quiet seems unnatural.

The quietest place on earth is reportedly in Building 87 at Microsoft's headquarters in Redmond, Washington. It's so quiet that the longest anybody has been able to bear it is forty-five minutes.[17] The chamber is so devoid of sound and echo that you can hear your own blood flowing through your veins, and your bones grinding as they move. It's unnerving. This is not what the monks of old were referring to, but it's how some people feel when they first attempt this discipline of silence. However, this discomfort slowly transitions to indescribable peace if you give it time. This carved-out space will soon become a conduit of grace, and perhaps your favorite few minutes of the day.

The practice of silence is letting all the buzz and noise of modern life dissipate so you can hear yourself think and listen to the voice of God—the still small voice. In our modern world, it's preciously hard to come by. And that's exactly what makes it so important.

One of my favorite Scripture verses is this one: "Be still and know that I am God" (Psalm 46:10).

Be still.

That's called silence. We need it now more than ever. The practice of silence stills the hum of distraction in our lives and allows our souls to breathe.

If we're going to access the power of silence, we need to be intentional in carving it out. We must prioritize it. It must be locked into our calendar.

The human heart was never designed to be bombarded with noise every second of the day, and silence is one of the only effective treatments for a strung-out soul.

SOLITUDE

Solitude is getting away from everyone—away from each and every person you know, including their digital avatars and social media selves. Solitude means silencing your email and turning off your phone—being unavailable to others for a time.

My wife and I share our house with our three amazing kids.

They're a ton of fun, but one thing they are *not* is quiet. Even with a decent sized home, it's impossible to find a place to truly be alone. I even built a room downstairs and finished it for Mel so she would have a place to get away and do her devotions in peace. Even that rarely works.

In a stroke of pure genius, friends of ours actually built a separate structure on their property out in the backyard to make space for solitude. They call it "Casita de Paz"—Spanish for "little house of peace." Solitude doesn't just happen, we need to prioritize it and seek it.

The positive effects of solitude seem to amplify when they're combined with nature. In my experience, getting out into the forest for a walk has a compounding effect.

Find a way to get away on a regular basis in your hectic life to restore the balance God designed us to live in. At its core, solitude is letting all the voices around you fade so you can hear the voice of God. The still small voice will not compete with the television and the train. It must be sought out.

FASTING

Fasting is giving up something good for something greater. This is what fasting represents at its core. Fasting is going without something you want or need, in order to take hold of something greater. Historically and biblically, this has often been food. In fact, in the pages of Scripture, the only examples of fasting relate to giving up food. But I've come to believe you can take the same principle and apply it to a multitude of things. In fact, fasting from digital distraction these days just might be as important.

Taking time away from our devices and our distractions and focusing that energy on our relationship with God and the relationships in our lives that matter most is our way of starving the weeds, drying them out. It's a way of halting their advance and stifling their growth.

I've heard many ways to meter this out. Some families take one hour a day off their phones. Others carve out meal time as a family affair with no digital presence allowed. Some choose one day a week to unplug. There are even braver souls among us who will choose one week a year to turn off their phones. As hard as it may be to believe, when they're done and the connection is broken, they're often not entirely sure they want to plug back in.

However you choose to do it, do something. Take a few minutes and make a start. At least build a small fence around what God is growing in you, and don't let anything else crowd it out.

These three disciplines are lifelines that God has given us to protect the abundant kind of life he's calling us to. Perhaps you should give them a try. Find a way to work them into your weekly and daily rhythm. Distraction will always find a way to be with us. But if we're intentional and mindful, we can guard ourselves from letting it choke out what really matters in life.

WEEDING YOUR GARDEN

So how do we know this lie is at work in our lives? Listen to Jesus. Look for weeds growing in your soul—it's the image he chose. Look for the thorns eating up your time, energy, and attention, and crowding out what really matters in your life.

What plants grow in the garden of your heart? Take a moment and think.

Time is the great equalizer. The richest man on earth gets twenty-four hours each day, and so do you and I. Billionaires have 86,400 seconds every time the earth spins, and you're allotted not a fraction less. The question is: How you will use that time?

Don't believe the lie, because it *does* matter what you do with your time and attention. If you've noticed your garden is overgrown, try the three lifelines discussed above. It has worked for the saints of old, and still has the power to transform your life.

10

The Lie of: **Passivity**

Life Is What Happens to You

> *I want you to know, my brothers, that what*
> *has happened to me has really served to advance*
> *the gospel… And because of this I rejoice.*
> PHILIPPIANS 1:12,18

I grew up watching the movie *The Princess Bride*. I've probably seen it half a dozen times. For the longest time, my wife was one of the few people in the world who could not stand that movie (though she has since seen the light). I've heard it quoted more times than just about any other movie from my childhood. If you've seen it, you may remember lines like "My name is Inigo Montoya, you killed my father, prepare to die!" The movie is chock full of other gems. One of them comes early in the story, as the hero Wesley tells his beloved, "Life is pain…. Anyone who says differently is selling something."

How's that for a mantra to live by? Wesley must have been the life of the party.

To be honest with you, I don't entirely agree with him. He's right in the sense that we ought to be wary of anyone who sells us a vision of the world that's all sunshine and rainbows, with no darkness or rain. However, life is full of far too many beautiful and wondrous things to write it off entirely. As we've discussed earlier, this world is beautiful and broken simultaneously, and any explanation of it has to include both.

But I do understand what Wesley was getting at. No matter how hard we try, we cannot escape the darker elements of reality. There are times when heartache and loss worm their way into our story, and sometimes in those moments, the pain is all we can see.

I've experienced many seasons like this—seasons of struggle and difficulty. I think most of us have. Whether it was the loss of a friendship, of a family member, or of a dream that was laid to rest, what I've learned is that many of us in the midst of these valleys end up believing a lie that prolongs our suffering and amplifies our pain. We believe the lie that life is simply what happens to you—that we're at the mercy of the circumstances of our lives.

At first glance, that may not seem all that misguided. In some respects it comes across like a statement of fact. After all, isn't life simply an accumulation of the things that have happened to us? But woven within that belief is a subtle untruth that distorts our reality.

The truth is, life is *not* just what happens to you. Life is *what you do with* what happens to you.

Those four little words have the power to change everything. Let me show you what I mean.

GOOD DAY, BAD DAY, WHO KNOWS?

There's an old Chinese proverb about a village farmer and his wife. They lived on the village outskirts with their son, and together they worked a plot of land held by their family for generations.

One day the farmer's only horse broke through the fence and ran away. He wasn't just the family pet; he was the only horsepower they owned. There was no John Deere in the barn to come to the rescue, and without him they would starve.

As soon as the neighbors heard of what happened, they came to the farmer to commiserate. "What a bad day this was,"

104

they said. "You don't have a horse for planting season! How will you feed your family?"

After listening to what they had to say, he replied, "Good day, bad day—who knows?"

A few days later, that same horse that had fled to the woods returned to his master, and with him he brought two more stallions. In that day and age, this was almost like winning the lottery. When his neighbors learned of it, they ran over to celebrate. You could hear their shouts as they approached. "Now you are a rich man!" they said. "What a fabulous day!"

The farmer listened again, and again he replied, "Good day, bad day—who knows?"

Later that day, the farmer's only son was thrown from one of the stallions and broke his leg. When the neighbors heard, they rushed over. "This is truly a bad day," they said. "Now you won't be able to plant your fields."

To which the farmer said, "Good day, bad day—who knows?"

The next morning the emperor's army rode into town to conscript the eldest son from every family. But the farmer's son with his broken leg was left behind, since he was unable to ride.

Soon the neighbors were back at his house, and tearfully they exclaimed, "Yours is the only son who was not taken and sent to war. What a good day for you!"

To which he replied (I'm sure you can guess), "Good day, bad day—who knows?"

I first heard this parable in my twenties, and in a beautiful way it illustrates the power of perspective. So many situations in our lives feel one way in the moment, but look entirely different in hindsight. Sometimes the most painful moments became the most powerful turning points in our story.

Let me ask you a question. The day that farmer's horse first ran away, was that a good day or a bad day? Which category does it belong to?

Well, it depends, doesn't it? It depends entirely on how you look at it. If all you're focused on is that small isolated situation, it truly was a terrible day. To lose your only means of making a living would be devastating, and if those twenty-four hours were all that mattered, it was without a doubt a tragedy.

But if you were to somehow take a step back and see the bigger picture—if you could zoom out and see the whole story simultaneously (the way that God sees everything)—your perspective would change, wouldn't it? From thirty thousand feet, this loss turned out to be the best possible thing that could have happened to him. Though he couldn't have known it at the time, that runaway horse would end up filling his barn and rescuing his son.

Here's the underlying question that has perpetually fascinated me: How exactly can one situation look so bad from one angle, and so good from another? It's the same situation, isn't it? It's the same horse, the same problem, and the same financial catastrophe.

Yet how you feel about it depends entirely on how you look at it. In other words, perspective is everything.

Perhaps the most powerful example of this is Good Friday. From one angle, it's the saddest moment in history. The sinless Son of God endured endless abuse and died while nailed to a cross. It was a moment of cosmic injustice with no equal. Yet we call it *Good* Friday. Why? Because through that injustice, Jesus ransomed the human race. It became the deepest form of good.

Actually, your whole life is like this. Your whole life is a choice about how you're going to look at the situations in front of you, and how you'll respond.

While I was growing up, my dad kept a quote posted on the wall of his office. In my memory I can still see it there, hanging alongside a few contractor jokes and newspaper clippings. Here's the quote: "Life is ten percent what happens to you, and ninety percent your attitude toward it."

I used to think this was one of those dime-a-dozen motivational clichés that usually have a wet cat hanging from a wire pictured above it, or a stunning mountain to climb. But after living through a few valleys of my own, I've come to realize that this is a profound biblical truth, one I had to learn the hard way.

THE POWER OF A FRAME

Chances are, in the room where you're reading this there's a picture frame hanging, slightly askew. What you may not realize is that this frame is a highly relevant analogy for the way you experience reality. Psychologists tell us that every time something happens to us, we put a frame around it, so to speak. We frame every situation we encounter in one way or another to help us understand and categorize what we're experiencing.

We do this automatically, without thinking. We put a frame around everything. That frame is constructed of an eclectic mixture of things: our emotions, our past experiences, our biases, our convictions, and the mood we woke up with that day. It's how we understand the world around us, and we use it every single day.

I live in a part of the country that has epic thunderstorms. We're not quite in tornado alley, but we do get some pretty dangerous and damaging storms. I didn't grow up here, so I still marvel at the dark clouds as they gather and the fury they can unleash. One day, not too long after God had called us here for ministry, we had a hailstorm to end all hailstorms. It was biblical in proportions. Sadly, my car was parked in the wide open space in front of my house. After the storm, it looked like it spent a month parked in the middle of a driving range. And it was going to cost several thousand dollars to fix. The timing for that was terrible—I was twenty-two and had just bought my first house, and Mel was going back to school.

What gives? Here I was, having moved across the country to follow God's call on my life—and this is how he repaid me!

It's so easy to get stuck in a frame of negativity like that. Sometimes that's the frame we reach for when something bad happens to us. We start to think, "Things like this always happen to me. I can never catch a break." We start to look at that event through a glass-half-empty kind of frame, focusing on all the things that aren't going our way. It can turn into an endless downward spiral.

Sometimes we reach for a victim frame. We look at a situation and think, "People are always taking advantage of me. I knew it! I knew they would do this to me." After the hailstorm, as I stared at my beaten up car, it felt like even the wind and the weather were against me. It's not just that hindsight is twenty/twenty, or that after something happens we tend to drastically overestimate what we think we already "knew" about it beforehand. Rather, this victim frame becomes the dominant way we view the events of our life. We get stuck in this mentality where the whole world is against us.

There's also a blame frame. When we reach for this one, we think, "I know exactly whose fault this is!" Whether it was your jerk of a boss, or that co-worker who never liked you, there's always someone to blame. I hate to admit it, but this is often my first reaction. When something bad happens, I instinctively seek someone to blame. If you're anything like me, you run through everything you would say if you ran into that person again. You rehearse the whole exchange, crafting every little punchline, until your brain melts under the weight of the imaginary conversation.

At other times we use a fear frame. This is where the majority of our worry comes from. We look at a single event and start to worry about all the other what-ifs that might take place. It's a kind of domino effect. How are we going to pay for this? What if we can't afford our mortgage? When we reach for a fear frame, all the other thoughts we have are infected with this kind of contagion. We look at that situation through fear goggles, and those lenses color our thoughts and emotions about everything.

Each of these examples are a type of frame. At one point or another, we've all reached for at least one of them. But you can also reach for a very different type of frame. When something difficult happens to us, we can choose to reach for a faith frame. We can let God frame the situation we're experiencing and begin to look at it the way he does—through the lens of eternity.

When you reach for a faith frame as you look at the difficult situation you're dealing with, your thoughts lean toward faith instead of fear. Instead of worrying about what might happen, or searching for someone to blame, you anchor your trust in God. You begin to think, "God will get me through this," and, "This is another opportunity for him to show me who he is!" Instead of dwelling on what might have been, or letting discouragement or bitterness root deeply in your soul, you begin to say, "I know this trial is hard, but I really do believe it will one day be a testimony!"

You start to remember what God has promised us: "All things work together for the good of those who love him and are called according to his purpose" (Romans 8:28). When you choose the faith frame, all of a sudden the same difficult experience looks and feels completely different.

As it turns out, God provided for my family more than we could have asked after that hailstorm in our first few years of ministry. The insurance company was not only nice to deal with (a miracle in its own right), they also paid us out more in hail damage than the car was actually worth. I couldn't see it at the time, but this was provision in disguise. Sometimes God will hide a blessing in a terrible situation, and you'll see it only in hindsight.

Do you see the power of a frame? It completely changes how you interact with reality. And what's amazing about all this is that *you*—not your circumstances—are in the driver's seat.

The truth is, you get to *choose* which frame you use. You may not be able to control what happens to you, but you can control how you react to it. You cannot control the ten percent of your circumstances, but you can control the ninety percent of your attitude toward it. In those situations, perspective is everything.

This is what we call *reframing*. It's the conscious choice to see the situation you're in from God's perspective instead of anyone else's. It's your choice to see it through the truth of Scripture, not just the emotion that rushes to the surface as you're experiencing it.

Paul was the king of reframing. I've seen it so often in his story, and I still marvel at his ability to reframe. Truthfully, if there's one thing he does in Scripture that I would like to learn, it's this—because I struggle with it every day.

BEHIND BARS

When he wrote his letter to the Philippians, Paul was in prison—again. He was in prison so often that if there was a frequent incarceration club, he would have been a platinum member. Here Paul was, cut off from the church he pastored and from everyone he loved. He was chained to a guard all day, and cold and lonely at night. He could have easily been depressed or angry. In some ways he had every right to be. At the very least you would think he would have been frustrated—I know I would have been. But instead, when you read Philippians, what does he say?

> I want you to know, my brothers, that what has happened to me has really served to advance the gospel... And because of this I rejoice. (Philippians 1:12,18)

When I read this, I almost feel like saying, "Paul, wake up! You're literally in chains! Look at the bars around you! You're cut off from the world and from everyone who cares about you! You're a missionary with no mission field!" That's how I would have felt. But Paul goes on:

> As a result, it has become clear throughout the whole palace guard and to everyone else that I am in chains for Christ. (1:13)

Do you see the frame he's using? Not the pessimist frame, or the blame frame, or the victim frame. Paul reaches for the faith frame. He essentially says, "I am not cut off, I have a captive audience!" I love this. "The soldier I'm chained to has to listen to me all day! Now all the soldiers have heard about Jesus, and the whole palace is buzzing with the gospel. If you think about it, this is the best thing that could have happened to me!"

The letter of Philippians is often called the Joy Letter, because some form of the word *joy* is used sixteen times in a few brief chapters. This is amazing, considering that Paul wrote this letter while surrounded by four stone walls of a prison, facing the very real chance that he was a dead man walking.

That's the power of a frame.

From one angle, Paul's life was hopeless and depressing. But from another, it was coursing with joy, because God had sneaked him into an amazing opportunity.

We need to learn to harness this power of reframing. Instead of being chained to our circumstances and at the mercy of what happens to us, we can rejoice in everything. Paul is proof of the fact that life isn't just what happens to you; it's *what you do* with what happens to you.

If you lose your job, you can allow that loss to crush you, or you can look at it and say, "This is another opportunity for God to provide for me. It will be a cool testimony that I'll tell my kids and grandkids one day." Perhaps it's an open door into new ministry and new possibilities.

If you break up with your boyfriend, you can allow those feelings of rejection to overwhelm you. Or you can remind yourself that God has a good plan for your life, and this wasn't it! Between you and me, I was brokenhearted in high school after my first real girlfriend broke up with me. At the time, it was everything. But now I actually thank God for the end of that relationship, because without it I never would have met my wife.

Again, the lie we battle here is that life is just what happens to you—and our first step in fighting back against it is to reframe those situations we don't want to be in. Reframe them with the truth that God has shown us in his Word. It will transform your thoughts and your emotions, because that's the power of a frame.

REJOICE

How exactly do we counter the narrative that our emotions want to tell us in those moments? One of the most powerful ways to accomplish this is to default to gratitude and praise.

Our world is waking up to the power of gratitude. You can read dozens of modern studies about the profoundly positive effects of being thankful instead of allowing discouragement to rule in your heart. But God has been teaching us this for thousands of years.

One of my favorite stories in the book of Acts is that of Paul and Silas in prison. That book is called Acts, which is short for "Acts of the Apostles," but really it should be "Acts of the Holy Spirit." God's Spirit is the driving force behind everything we read in Acts. He is the real missionary.

Paul and Silas are in prison—again. This time because they had the audacity to cast a demon out of a slave girl who was making her master a ton of money telling fortunes. When she was released from this evil spirit, she no longer had insight into the spiritual world, so her owners had Paul and Silas thrown in jail for their lost income.

Here they were, bound and chained. Their feet were in stocks. They were being held in an inner cell which was the prison's maximum security ward. It was the hardest place to escape from. Moreover, they had been severely flogged—beaten by rods and whips.

It was midnight (everything seems worse in the black of night, doesn't it?), and Paul and Silas were in pain. Their situation seemed hopeless. And what did they do? Did they complain? Did they let despair overwhelm them? Did they vow to quit this whole apostle thing if they ever made it out of this mess?

No. They started singing.

This moment in time never gets old for me. I can picture it as if I'm there with them. In the dark of night, in the depths of a prison, there sounded songs of thanksgiving and praise. Quiet at first, then ascending in volume and conviction. Luke tells us that the other inmates leaned into the sound and could hear them throughout the place. Their sonorous melodies echoed off the cold stone walls and through the iron bars in every direction.

Craig Groeschel retells this scene with a bit of theatrical license. For me, it puts flesh on a powerful story:

Paul: Hey, Si…

Silas: Yeah?

Paul: We're not dead!

Silas: That's true, Paul.

Paul: So I was thinking—if we're not dead, we're not done!

Silas: That's right!

Paul: You know what else? Our God is still on the throne!

Jesus is risen and at the right hand of the Father, and he's praying for us!

Silas: Yes!

Paul: I think we need to give him a little praise. What do you want to sing?[18]

And so they filled that prison with songs of thanksgiving. Whether or not those two could sing, I guarantee you it was one of the most beautiful sounds ever heard, and no one in that jail ever forgot it.

Maybe you're wondering what they were praising God for. It's a fair question. Why would they praise when they were still surrounded by bars and gates? In that moment, they were praising God for who he is, not just for what he was doing right then and there. They were remembering his character, his goodness, and his love for them. They were leaning toward the grace of God, which is closely linked in Greek to what the word *rejoice* means.[19] They were worshiping a God they knew was good, even if life didn't feel good for them in the moment.

But that wasn't all. They were also praising God for what he was *about* to do. They didn't know it yet, but an earthquake was on the way. God had scheduled some divine tectonic activity. He was about to shake the very ground they were standing on and shatter the iron doors that held them captive. In just a matter of moments, the prison would be rocked by the hand of God Almighty, and the bars would be torn from their hinges while the whole prison went into revival. The jailer and his family were moments away from the waters of baptism! God was on his way, but Paul and Silas began to praise him before he showed up.

They praised God *before* the victory![20]

Usually that's not how it works, is it? Usually we pray for God to show up, then praise him after he does. But what if praise is actually what unlocks the power of God in our lives? What if there's immense power in praising God *before* the victory? Not only does he step into the situation we're facing, but he changes our hearts while we wait.

Reframe and rejoice. It's an unbeatable combination. Reframe the situation you're in, and consciously choose a different frame to use. Then rejoice in who God is and in what he's about to do. That's how we fight against this lie in our lives, and remove the leverage the enemy is using against us.

Refuse to be chained to your circumstances.

Refuse to let them own you.

PREACHING TO THE PASTOR

Last year I was in the middle of a rough season. I'll spare you the details, but it was one of those situations when the pressure of a whole bunch of circumstances crested at once.

I wasn't the only one feeling the tension. Lately, everyone's baseline for stress has reached a high watermark. Meanwhile, on top of whatever particular crisis each person might be facing, life still goes on. There's still the stress of parenting and work and trying to juggle all our commitments, not to mention the stress of finances and the unpredictability of life. My own situation was a concoction of several of these, and the cauldron was ready to boil over.

I came home one day to vent to my wife about it. When you're as verbal as I am, it sure helps to have a wife who's a great listener. We took a personality test once, and it turns out that in this area, we could not be more different (actually in a lot of areas, it seems). I'm in the 99th percentile of what they call expressiveness (which is all about how verbal you are)—and my wife is in the 4th percentile. Translation: I talk a lot—more than 99 percent of people—while Mel is really good at listening. That night, as I was telling her how frustrated I was, she stopped me and said, "Okay, but are you praising God in the middle of it?"

I stopped and thought, *Pardon me?* I was a bit stunned. That wasn't how this usually went. Usually my lovely wife would listen to me vent, then put her hand on my shoulder and say "There, there," or something like it. This time she was pushing back.

I answered, "I don't feel like praising God right now. I'm actually a little mad at him!" (Have you ever felt that before?)

But she kept pushing, and I was growing genuinely frustrated with her. If you've ever met my wife, you would know she's one of the sweetest persons alive, and you'd never think it was possible to be mad at her. But trust me, it is! (Which, by the way says a lot more about me than her.)

I felt like saying, "Back off! I don't want to thank God for this!" Real mature, I know. *Way to go, pastor.*

In that conversation, she retold me this exact story about Paul and Silas, and explained to me that we need to praise God *before* the victory, not just afterward. She reminded me that I should be doing this even now, when I didn't feel like it. Perhaps especially now.

As she was talking, I was thinking *Wow, that's good. I should write that down.* But I couldn't let her know she was winning. (Have you ever been wrong in a fight, but kept swinging even after you'd lost? We all have our moments.)

The next morning I woke up, made my way to the church, closed all the sanctuary doors, and turned on the sound system. I played praise and worship music through the speakers as if it was Sunday morning. I sang along and had a worship service, with just me present—which, if you've heard me sing, is probably not a bad thing.

For the first song, my arms were still crossed, and so was my heart. It didn't come immediately. But by the second song I could feel something starting to shift in me. I could feel the inclination of my heart changing inside me. And after a few minutes, I realized my wife was right. My heart flooded with grace. My whole perspective began to change. The prison walls of my soul began to shake, and the gates began to break free.

That is the power of gratitude. That is the power of praise.

If we're willing to praise God before the victory, and thank him for what he's about to do, there's no prison cell that can hold you.

Reframe and rejoice. Start today. You'll never go back. You won't ever want to.

Pay attention to the frame you're using.

And remember: Life isn't what happens to you. It's what you do with what happens to you.

11

The Lie of:
Temptation

God Is Holding Out on You

*No temptation has overtaken you except what is
common to mankind. And God is faithful; he will
not let you be tempted beyond what you can bear.
But when you are tempted, he will also provide a
way out so that you can endure it.*
1 CORINTHIANS 10:13

grew up with some very wealthy friends. I guess that's what
happens when you attend a private Christian school. My family was solidly middle class, but some very successful people sent
their kids to our high school, and they became some of my closest
friends. One of them lived in a four-story house (with two staircases), situated on eight river lots. Not exactly roughing it.

We were hanging out at his place one day, which had nothing to do with the fact that his mom was one of the best cooks
in town, and his parents asked me to run an errand for them. It
was nothing fancy, just a supply run, and they handed me their
Visa card to cover the costs. It wasn't until later that night that I
opened my wallet and realized I'd forgotten to give it back.

It's not often a sixteen-year-old opens up his wallet and
finds a shiny new Visa card staring back at him. It's a moment
you savor. This kind of thing was new for me. It turns out this
wasn't just any Visa; it was a no-limit premium gold card! The

kind of card you can walk in and swipe for a brand new car, and drive out.

I remember just staring at the card. Watching it glint in the overhead street lights. It was almost luminescent. My friends saw me caught in its spell, and quickly put the pieces together.

It didn't take long for the atmosphere to shift from awe to action. They started shouting instructions at me: "Go buy us a pizza!" "Never mind, go buy us two pizzas!" "Then let's go to Dairy Queen!" Clearly we weren't criminal masterminds. All we could think of when we had a blank check was fast food and DQ. Over and over they plied me with suggestions and begged me to use my not-quite-stolen card.

At first I didn't say anything; I was still in shock.

But they kept on pushing. "Go and spend it!" "This will be so much fun!" "They'll never notice." "Come on man, they're loaded! They won't even miss a dime of it!"

They were relentless.

You've seen the man with an angel on one shoulder and the devil on the other? Arguing about what to do next? Well, that night I had four of them whispering in my ear. Begging me to give in.

Temptation comes in many forms, but if you look closely enough, the lies surrounding it are remarkably similar. It's always some variation of the same line. It's always a promise of pleasure, and an assurance of immunity. Right? Whatever "that" is will always be fun! And don't worry, no one will even notice.

That same voice will drag you through the mud if you ever give in. But until then, it's all smiles and promises.

Thankfully, I was strong enough that night to resist. My friends were inconsolable. I shook them off my back and returned the card to its rightful owner. That family had been so good to me, I just couldn't repay their kindness with theft.

But I haven't always been so successful in the face of

temptation. I don't think any of us have. In fact, many of us are stuck in a loop of temptation, shame, and confession—not entirely sure how to climb out.

There's a lie at the heart of every temptation, regardless of what that specific temptation is. It's a lie we buy into every single time we give in. Temptation is always infused with so much desire and emotion, it's hard to believe we're doing any thinking at all in those moments, but we are. The lie that we've been sold as we stand at those crossroads is this: *God is holding out on you.*

That's what we come to believe, if only for a moment—that God knows what's best for you, but he has fenced it off, and so you'll be better off by giving in.

This was the story of Genesis 3, a story that continues to repeat itself throughout our lives. Remember how the serpent sold the apple to Eve? Remember the pitch? It was for wisdom, the serpent promised. It was to know the difference between right and wrong. Why wouldn't God want us to have that?

But it was an invitation built on a lie. Temptation is that whisper in your ear that even though God said *this*, you'll actually be happier if you do *that* instead.

Once you believe the lie that God is holding out on you, everything starts to change.

At its heart, temptation is an invitation to do something you know is wrong—and to do it for a reason that feels right. The problem is that the promise is all style and no substance. The tempter will promise you the world, then disappear when you come to collect.

RIGHT DESIRE, WRONG PATH

The enemy has no real power of creation, but only of corruption. He's limited to twisting the good things God has made. So when he tempts us, he's actually inviting us to meet a genuine God-given desire in some other way than what God has provided. In other words, all temptation is essentially the *right desire*—but the *wrong path*.

You could be forgiven if you thought it was more complicated than that, but it really is that simple. Right desire, wrong path.

God has created us with deep desires and needs. Those are the magnetic draws and emotional instincts that drive most of our decisions. There are desires for community, connection, love, fulfillment, and respect. Desire for meaning, joy, and pleasure. These are all good desires—godly desires, in fact. God created us with them, and he intended us to have them.

But that wasn't all. He also provided a means to meet them, each in their respective way. He provided a path to their fulfillment. Temptation is the twisting of that created order. It's the invitation to meet those needs yourself, in any way other than the means God provided.

Let me give you an example. Marriage was God's plan for us from the beginning. In fact, he officiated the very first wedding. God has an amazing plan for our sexual fulfillment, our desire for kids, and our first and in some ways fundamental unit of community. God is all for sex. It was his idea. This is all good in every sense of the word.

Right desire, right path.

Temptation, on the other hand, promises you the pleasure of sex without the energy and involvement of commitment. It's a shortcut. Whether it's the lure of pornography or sex before marriage, each shortcut is an invitation to meet that desire outside the channel God has created. Usually it's a quick and easy way around, but it always ends the same way: drama and trauma. That's the result of charting a path other than the one God has laid out.

Just look around. The sexual revolution of the sixties promised us freedom, and all it produced was dysfunction.

Never forget: If there's a good and godly desire, there's a correspondingly good and godly path to meet it. It's not always easy to see, and rarely instant, but it's the only path that leads to fulfillment.

The truth is, God isn't holding out on us. In fact, he's trying to lead us to the very thing we're desperate for, while protecting us from hollow pursuits.

I've reflected on the following quote from C. S. Lewis for years, and it rings true every time:

> It would seem that our Lord finds our desires not too strong, but too weak. We are half-hearted creatures, fooling about with drink and sex and ambition when infinite joy is offered us, like an ignorant child who wants to go on making mud pies in a slum because he cannot imagine what is meant by the offer of a holiday at sea. We are far too easily pleased.[21]

Temptation is always a trade: something lesser for something greater. A moment of pleasure in exchange for lasting peace. But what if God wants all these things for you far more than you want them for yourself? What if the Bible isn't a book of restrictions, but a treasure map for those willing to seek? As the psalmist wrote, "I rejoice in your word like one who discovers a great treasure" (Psalm 119:162 NLT).

THE PERFECT TRAP

Understanding the nature of temptation is half the battle. But if you're anything like me, you need a little more help in this fight. Once we remove this lie from our heart and replace it with the truth that God is genuinely looking out for our best interests, it has a way of disarming those future encounters and laying bare the false promises that temptation makes.

But sometimes it's not just information we need, but application. We need a way to put it into practice. This truth needs handles. After all, the single greatest distance in the world is the distance from our head to our heart.

So I want to sift through the story of temptation we find in Genesis 39. It's a masterclass of sorts. Second only to what we see in Christ's temptation in the desert, it's perhaps the clearest roadmap in Scripture to overcoming the lures of temptation.

Whether your battle right now is a New York cheesecake sitting in the fridge, or a boyfriend you know you shouldn't see, this story is a story of victory. And it's a story we desperately need. In this part of Scripture, God lays out a strategy of sorts. It's a simple plan that Joseph seemed to intuitively carry into battle, and which delivered him each and every time—a plan with three parts.

REFUSE

You may know the backstory. Betrayed by his brothers and sold into slavery, Joseph wound up in Potiphar's house. With God's hand upon him, Potiphar gave him ever increasing responsibility, and soon he climbed the prison ladder and was put in charge of everything. If you wanted to summarize Joseph's story, you could do it in three words: he went from a pit, to a prison, to a palace—all in about thirteen years.

But it wasn't just Potiphar who took notice of Joseph—Potiphar's wife was just as enamored. She approached him day after day and invited him to sleep with her. The word *brazen* comes to mind—she was bold and without shame.

How did Joseph respond to her constant invitation and the whispers of temptation? It's right there in the text:

> Now Joseph was well-built and handsome, and after a while his master's wife took notice of Joseph and said, "Come to bed with me!" *But he refused.* (Genesis 39:6-8)

There are many parts of Scripture that seem a bit understated. Sometimes a profound truth gets only three words—as it does here. If you're underwhelmed, I get it. At first I was too. This doesn't sound like much of a master plan at first glance, but there's more here than you might think. When it comes to temptation, this is always step one. Your first and often most effective line of defense is to shut the door as soon as it opens. This is what James (the brother of Jesus) was getting at when he said, "Resist the devil and he will flee from you" (James 4:7).

I can imagine you sitting there and saying to yourself, "What kind of advice is that? *Just say no?* If it were that easy, none of us would be in this mess! I've said no a thousand times and it has never worked!"

But the problem for many of us is not that we didn't say no, but that *we said it too late*. It was more of an afterthought. Our no followed a lengthy period of consideration where we thought it through and weighed the pros and cons. We tried saying no after testing the water first, wading in up to our knees. The problem is, by that point the crocodiles already know where you are. When I've fallen, it has always been the times when my no was too late.

It's like the difference between a snowball and an avalanche. Imagine a snowball at the top of a mountain. Picture a pristine, white-capped Rocky Mountain peak. Now it's easy to stop a snowball at the top of a mountain before it rolls down, isn't it? All you do is pick it up when it's small and slow. When it drops to the ground and begins to roll, it's no bigger than your hands—even a child could scoop it up. But if you let it get some momentum—if you let it gather speed and mass—then downslope it will run you over like a freight train, with all the inertia of an avalanche.

Temptation functions much the same. Once it's been given space to run, it will destroy everything in its wake. It gathers strength with time and repetition. Joseph's example to us all is to pick that snowball up when it's small—to say no right at the crest of the mountain. Distract yourself or walk away. Don't give the temptation time and space to grow.

For Joseph, this worked.

Until it didn't…

REFOCUS

Joseph's story also reveals his second strategy in fighting temptation: to step back and refocus. Nearly all the strategies Joseph employs in this fight are in-the-moment strategies. They're the "in case of emergency, break glass" kind of plans. I find them so incredibly useful because temptation rarely comes with advance warning.

Step one was to close the door. But if she barges through, step two is to take a step back. When Potiphar's wife propositioned Joseph again, hear what he said:

> "With me in charge," he told her, "my master does not concern himself with anything in the house; everything he owns he has entrusted to my care. No one is greater in this house than I am. My master has withheld nothing from me except you, because you are his wife. How then could I do such a wicked thing and sin against God?" And though she spoke to Joseph day after day, he refused to go to bed with her or even be with her. (Genesis 39:8-10)

Listen carefully to Joseph's response. When she propositioned him, he immediately started talking about her husband, Potiphar! Talk about a mood killer. His first topic of conversation was the man who would be devastated by her offer. And Joseph didn't stop there. He went on and on about how great her husband was, how worthy of respect, and how wonderful he'd been to Joseph. I assure you, that really would have killed the vibe Potiphar's wife was working toward.

Then Joseph started talking about God. He reminded her that God was watching, and that this would be both a wicked thing and a cold-blooded sin.

Honestly, it was brilliant. I can guarantee you that half the infidelities in America would never occur if someone invited all the affected parties into the conversation in a moment like this.

Watch this drama unfold, we see an ever increasing circle of cast members. At first there were just two people in the room—Joseph and Potiphar's wife. But now, through the mention that Joseph makes, there are four. Count them: The two of them, plus her husband, and the God of the universe. All would be affected by this choice.

What makes this second strategy so effective is the way it counters the fundamental nature of temptation. Temptation is always myopic—it always has tunnel vision. Temptation is always about the here and now—that's it. "It's just us," she says. "Just now! Live in the moment! Who cares about tomorrow!" I've gotten to the point that if I hear one more song on the radio preaching a message like this, I'm going to stick a screwdriver into it. The truth is, it's never just her and him, is it? A lot of people are affected by their choice. So many people's futures hang in the balance.

Joseph refused to buy the lie that all that matters is now. He refused to get focused on this tiny moment in time, on this sliver of history.

He took a step back, and refocused. He cleared his head. That's how Joseph got the perspective he needed. *He remembered tomorrow today.*

Sure, *it's just one shady business deal, right? It's just one x-rated website. It's just one little lie.* That's what we tell ourselves. *It's just one solitary choice.*

But what if it's not? What if it's the first among many? What if they aren't just individual actions, but steps on a path? What if the consequences of this choice or this action will reverberate for a lifetime?

Choices are cumulative. They're summative. What if the destination of that path was destruction? The destruction could have been averted if there had been a simple course correction at the start.

So shut the door. Refuse. Immediately. If it pushes open, take a step back and refocus—get the big picture.

RUN

When all else fails, *run*. Run as fast and as far as you can. I don't mean spiritually distance yourself from the situation, or whatever that means. I mean physically find the nearest exit and run for your life! Joseph left so fast he left his coat behind. It's my favorite image in the entire story.

When this likely young and gorgeous woman cornered him in her room and threatened to have him jailed if he refused, Joseph had one last option. Realizing the danger he was in, Joseph hit the eject button and got out as fast as he could. That's how you conquer temptation.

Running is not a sign of weakness; it's a sign of wisdom and strength. We all have friends who influence us to make poor choices, or circumstances that typically make us fall. We've all been in situations where bad decisions fill the air. Joseph shows us that when all else fails—if you know the walls are closing in— don't reason with it; just run! It's our last line of defense.

NEVER SETTLE

So let's fast-forward to the present. Joseph's story gives us the tools to fight back, but your fight likely isn't with a rich heiress in a riverside palace. You have your own battles to wage. Where do you need to apply this most? What arena of temptation have you been the least successful in? Where has this lie that God is holding out on you taken hold?

A. W. Tozer famously wrote, "What comes into our minds when we think about God is the most important thing about us."[22] I couldn't agree more. Our view of the character and nature of God affects every part of our life. It affects how we view everything else around us—including temptation.

So many of us, along with our culture at large, are caught in the lie that God is holding out on us. Someone has convinced us that God doesn't really want what's best for us. This lie—this false view of God—is robbing us of our freedom. Don't let it root down in your soul. Remember, God *always* has your best interests at heart.

What you really want is the right thing on the right path. Never settle for a cheap substitute.

REMEMBER THE HOOK

So what do we look for when we're faced with temptation? What's our sign that we're in trouble? Our sign is a hook. Remember the hook.

One of the words for temptation in the New Testament is *deleazo,* which literally means to bait a hook, or to lure. In Greek, it's a fishing term. The art of fishing hasn't changed much in a thousand years. You simply find something desirable (to a fish) and hide a hook in it. It's that simple. You don't let the fish see the hook; all they see is the bait. But as soon as they bite down, you reel them in. This method is as old as time.

I don't know what you find desirable, but my guess is that it's not worms or cut bait. Perhaps it's a freshly baked Cinnabon roll, fresh out of the oven—covered in butter and icing. That smell in the mall is irresistible. Every time I go, I feel like the cartoon character floating away on its vapor trail. Or maybe baked goods aren't your weakness; how about a thousand dollar bill? Would that grab your attention if I offered you one?

What kind of bait catches your eye? Think about it. And remember this: All temptations are the same. Regardless of what the bait is, underneath is a hook—always. So the next time you're tempted—when you hear that little voice on your shoulder, or those thoughts pop into your head promising you the time of your life with no regrets—remember the hook. It's there, though you can't see it. And nothing is worth the price of getting hooked by it.

12

The Lie of:
Unforgiveness

Holding On to the Hurt Won't Hurt You

*Get rid of all bitterness, rage and anger, brawling
and slander, along with every form of malice. Be
kind and compassionate to one another, forgiving
each other, just as in Christ God forgave you.*
Ephesians 4:31-32

I was eight years old when I got my first black eye. Most kids manage to earn their first shiner in an accidental encounter with a coffee table, or a collision with a sibling, but mine was in a schoolyard fight.

I say fight, but that may be a tad misleading. The truth is, my opponent was three years older than me and twice my size. He ended things in a single blow. I was walking home from school, and had reached the corner of my street when someone tapped me on the shoulder. As I turned around, all I saw was a huge mitt headed straight for my face. Then nothing. Everything went black. I wish I could tell you I took it like a champ, but the truth is I dropped like a sack of potatoes.

I'd somehow upset the wrong sixth grader, and he followed me home to settle the score. This was my welcome to the real world—where not everyone is your friend, and sometimes people do some pretty awful things to you for no apparent reason. I ran home crying trying to make sense of what just happened.

That may have been the first time I remember anyone hurting me in a very real way, but it wasn't the last. Truthfully, life is full of experiences like this. When you live in a broken world full of broken people, it's only a matter of time until you get cut on one of the sharp edges. And here's the real question in all of this: When (not "if") that happens, what are you going to do next?

At the end of the day, we really have only two choices when someone wrongs us: hold on, or let go. I wish I could give you a few more options, but those are it. We can release it, or we can let it metastasize and become a part of us. Ultimately we end up choosing one or the other.

There's a lie that many of us have come to believe. It's so common these days that we rarely question it. It's a lie that's been passed down from generation to generation, and it's so well accepted today that few ever bother to address it. It's the lie that says when you've been wronged, you can hold on to the hurt without it hurting you.

I'm not sure we even process this lie on an intellectual level. Most of this kind of thinking is done deep within the wells of our emotions. But at the end of the day, the promise goes something like this: Bottle it up until you can pour it back out. Don't let that other person get away with it. You can make this right—just dish it right back.

Don't get mad; get even.

When we're wounded, something deep inside of us demands that we make it right, and often we hold on to that pain until the score has been settled. That's what makes us such easy prey for this deception. We buy into the lie that it's actually possible to hold on to the hurt without it hurting us.

RAT POISON

The church I pastor is right on the edge of town. Thirty years ago, the place where the church building stands was a cornfield. The location is beautiful, and the building campaign was a miracle, but there's one small thing I would love to change. Mice. Far too many of them. Every year, especially in the fall, we have visitors—not the good kind of visitors, but the tiny furry ones with beady little eyes.

Though it's a relatively new building, they still find a way in. I'm told they can fit through a gap as small as an eighth of an inch. Our resident director, Lorna, is the one who takes the brunt of their annual invasion.

Our church has a dynamic drama ministry, and often puts on full-length theatrical plays. In the loft there are tons of large paper-mache stones—the kind that makes you look like Hercules when you pick one up. And every year, somehow these little rodents find their way in, climb up to the second story, and chew holes through Jesus's tomb. It's infuriating.

These fabricated rocks are made of flour and water stretched across a metal frame, and apparently mice find it irresistible. When all is said and done, the only thing they leave behind is a chicken wire skeleton. Every year the furry little creatures make their annual pilgrimage upstairs to a Thanksgiving feast.

This recurring battle reminds me of something Anne Lamott once said: "Unforgiveness is like eating rat poison and waiting for the rat to die."[23] I still believe this to be about the most insightful parallel I've ever read. Holding on to the hurt that someone else has caused you is precisely that toxic. At the end of the day, the rats will carry on, doing what they always do. And ultimately, the person you're hurting the most is yourself.

Despite the lie we've been sold, the truth is that when we won't let go of the evil someone else has done to us, we're the ones who end up paying the highest price.

PARABLE OF THE UNMERCIFUL SERVANT

Jesus tells a parable in Matthew 18 that deals with this reality. It's a story of forgiveness, of what happens inside us when we refuse to let go. Jesus tells it in response to a question Peter raises, one that perhaps you, too, have wondered: "How many times shall I forgive my brother when he sins against me?" Or perhaps in our day and age: "How many second chances are people entitled to?"

Before I give you Jesus's answer, let me ask you: How many times should you forgive someone before you throw in the towel? How many times do you let someone wound you the same way before you close the door? Think back on your own life. What's your breaking point?

In Peter's question, he gives Jesus a starting point, almost as if trying to answer his own question. He jumps all the way up to seven: "Lord, how many times shall I forgive my brother or sister who sins against me? Up to seven times?" (Matthew 18:21).

The number seven is actually remarkable. The consensus among rabbis at the time was that a brother could be forgiven for a sin up to three times, but three was enough. That was the ceiling, not the floor. So when Peter hears Jesus's teaching on forgiveness, and realizes just how important forgiveness is in the Lord's view—he more than doubles what everyone agrees is the limit.

But Jesus comes back with a number so far beyond comprehension, it's impossible even to imagine. It's not three, or seven, but seventy-seven times; and some translations say seven times seventy—which is 490 acts of forgiveness! I hope somebody caught Peter when he fainted.

Now, if you're numerically inclined, does Jesus mean that if we crossed the line and hit 491, then we're off the hook? No. As N. T. Wright comments, "If you're still counting how many times you've forgiven someone, you're not really forgiving them. Just postponing revenge."[24] Therefore Jesus, as he often does, tells a story to drive his point home.

This story is of a king who wanted to settle accounts. He called in his servants, one of whom owed the king an unimaginable sum. The number in Scripture is measured in gold, and it would have exceeded ten thousand pounds of it. Based on today's going rate, that's worth more than three hundred million dollars, give or take.

The servant of course was unable to make good on his bill, so the king pronounced judgment: The servant and all his family would be sold into slavery.

At once the servant fell to his knees and begged for mercy. He swore he would pay back the money if he could just be given a little more time. And the king, being kind and generous, went one step further and forgave the whole amount.

Like a man just taken off death row, the servant leaped for joy and ran off, not waiting around to see if the king would change his mind. Along the way, he happened to meet a friend who owed him money—an amount that was only a small fraction of the sum the king had just written off. The servant grabbed his friend, choked him, and demanded immediate payment. The friend refused, so the servant had him thrown in jail, to be kept there until the debt was repaid.

Those who knew that servant were greatly upset by this outrageous behavior, which they reported to the king. The king's fury boiled over. He summoned the servant and gave him a tongue-lashing, then sent him off to be kept in prison until every last red cent he'd ever owed was paid off.

It's not hard to see where Jesus is going with this. God has forgiven us for a colossal debt—for our every sin, misdeed, hurtful word, and selfish action—a lifetime's worth of wrong. Yet often when we're faced with the option to forgive our brothers or sisters for a solitary wound, or a single mistake, we resist and refuse.

Listen again to N. T. Wright:

Forgiveness is like the air in your lungs. There's only room for you to inhale the next lungful when you've just breathed out the previous one. If you insist on withholding it, refusing to give someone else the kiss of life they may desperately need, you won't be able to take any more in yourself.[25]

When we withhold forgiveness, we block from our experience the very thing that has given us life.

We're to forgive because we've been forgiven. It's that simple. You simply can't receive it without giving it—otherwise, there's no room.

WHERE'S THE HAPPY ENDING?

Now, if you're like me, you're probably uncomfortable with how this parable of the king and his servant ends. If you read the Gospels, Jesus doesn't seem to have the same need for happy endings that we do. This idea of the jailers torturing the man until he pays back what he owes is uncomfortable at best.

But what if that detail was prophetic? What if Jesus was trying to tell us something? What if, when we hold on to unforgiveness, we actually give the enemy free rein to make us suffer?

Paul talks about a foothold we give the enemy in our lives, and it centers on the times others have wounded us:

"In your anger do not sin": Do not let the sun go down while you are still angry, and do not give the devil a foothold. (Ephesians 4:26-27)

Not only is it a lie that we can hold on to that hurt without it harming our own soul, quite the opposite is true. Holding on to an offense is like hanging a vacancy sign on your heart and inviting the devil to come right in and make your life miserable.

Our refusal to release each other is a formal invitation for our enemy to chain us to that event. We give him permission to make us relive that moment over and over for the rest of our lives. When you hold on to the anger and the pain, the moment never dies. It's endlessly resurrected. It's new every morning, with a fresh store of energy.

Unforgiveness holds us captive, like a prison—except that this prison is locked from the inside.

I'm convinced that very few of us make this choice consciously. Normal people don't sit down in the morning and make a mental list of their ongoing grudges as they sip their coffee. I've met a few of those people, and so have you, but they're the exception. For many of us, however, when we've been wronged, we simply can't let go. We feel chained to those moments no matter how much time has passed.

I've thought about the why behind that reality for many years. Why can't we let go? Why does that pain often turn into resentment as time passes? After counseling dozens of people through it, I believe that most people today simply don't understand the biblical concept of forgiveness. Instead they have these caricatures and faulty pictures of forgiveness in their minds, and these very pictures have held them back from the only decision with the power to set them free.

Let me see if I can explain through a real life story.

LIFELONG DREAMS

My friend Shea had a lifelong dream of opening his own restaurant. He had an inherent gift for hospitality and a knack for business, so it was a natural fit. He even had a name for his restaurant picked out years earlier—Chaise Café. It sounded exactly like what it was, Shea's Café—witty and winsome all at the same time.

When he'd finally lined up the financing and found a location, it was a bit of a dream come true. He tapped every resource he possibly could to achieve liftoff. We were there with his family for his soft launch, and I've never seen him so tired and happy at once.

That first year was a whirlwind. He was never quite sure if he was coming or going. For the most part, things went as well as he could have hoped—until he found out his manager was stealing from him.

It started off as a few dollars from the till, and some unrecorded meals. But then there were duplicate checks, each for thousands of dollars. By the time he uncovered the theft, he realized that his manager was planning to steal nearly $50,000 that year alone—from a young entrepreneur who was trying to keep his business afloat in the precarious first year. Truthfully, it could have been the death of the dream Shea had nurtured since high school.

Now let's ask the question: What does forgiveness look like here? Does forgiveness mean my friend should rehire his thieving manager? Is that what Jesus is calling him to? Should he offer him his old job back and tell him the new alarm codes and banking passwords?

I think we all know the answer to that. It's an unequivocal no. That would be foolishness. It's not noble; it's naive. But many of us confuse that with forgiveness, which brings us to our first caricature: Forgiveness is *not* being a doormat.

There's this natural assumption many of us carry around that if we forgive someone, we're essentially allowing them to walk all over us again. It's almost as if we're giving them permission to continue whatever behavior that wounded us so deeply in the first place. Let me be clear: This is not what forgiveness means.

Forgiveness is a choice to let go; it is *not* letting ourselves be taken advantage of again, or ignoring the warning signs we've come to know so well. When Jesus exhorts us to forgive one another, he isn't asking us to allow people to use and abuse us again and again. There are absolutely times when you'll be hurt by someone you've forgiven before, but forgiveness is not an invitation to be a doormat. Rather, it's a choice to let go of the pain, and let God be God in our situations.

Second, forgiveness is *not* minimizing what happened to you. This is another caricature we struggle against. For my friend to pretend it wasn't a big deal to jeopardize the one thing he'd poured his life into would be dishonest on a level hard to imagine. Often we assume this is what forgiveness looks like—to play it off like it was nothing.

Now sometimes, perhaps, that is true. Not every slope is a hill we need to die on. There are things we should simply let roll off our backs. But often the offense was *not* merely "nothing," was it? Sometimes it was, in fact, a big deal. There are real wounds and real consequences attached to the wrongs that have been committed against us, and the path to forgiveness does not lead through Minimization Valley—the place where you pretend that the issue or the event was insignificant.

The real path to forgiveness actually *requires* that we don't minimize the pain. You'll see why in a moment. We must count the actual cost.

Neither of those two caricatures is a true picture of forgiveness, and you cannot let them cloud your vision.

MORE THAN A FEELING

This is probably the most important thing I'll say in this chapter. It's the truth that, for me, flipped this whole experience on its head.

Forgiveness is *not* a feeling; *forgiveness is a choice.*

Take a moment to read that sentence again. We often say stuff like, "Oh, I'm not ready to forgive"—as if it's our emotion that must eventually change. We hope that something will magically wash over us when the appointed number of days has passed, and we'll finally be able to let go. We've been told time heals all wounds, and we're hoping that's right.

But the dark reality of unforgiveness is that if you continue to feed it, it will outlive you. If you wait to feel like forgiving someone, you may never arrive.

This is where the distinction comes into play. Forgiveness is not a function of the emotions, but of the will. It's something you *choose*. This is why Jesus can command it. Feelings are not within our complete control, but choices are. At its heart, forgiveness is choosing not to take revenge for what someone else has done to you.

It's that simple.

It's making the choice *not* to make them pay. It's neither being naive, nor minimizing the pain, nor waiting for a better feeling to arrive. It's a choice you make to let the offending person off your hook. That's it.

If you're anything like me, as soon as someone tells you forgiveness is letting someone off your hook, there's a deep-seated part of you that will cry foul. Trust me, I feel it too. There's something that rises up in all of us that says, "That's not fair!"

But hear it again: Forgiveness is the choice you make to let the offending person off *your* hook. They're never off God's hook. He'll deal with them justly and without bias—which is something you and I could never hope to achieve. "Vengeance is mine, says the Lord" (Romans 12:19)—vengeance is never yours nor mine.

When you choose to forgive someone, you're saying, "I won't make you pay for what you've done. I won't give you the cold shoulder every time I pass by. I won't fail to invite you when there are meetings at work. I won't talk behind your back and litigate this issue until everyone's on my side."

I *will* let go.

Forgiveness may be hard, but at its heart it isn't complicated. Years ago I learned a method that has helped me dozens of times. It's a physical way to work through the spiritual reality. I teach it to my church on a regular basis, and if you want to find a way to let go, you can try these three steps:

1. *Write an I.O.U.* The first step is to identify who exactly has hurt you. It may be a very long list. I've often sat with a pen and paper, closed my eyes, and prayed, "Lord, who do I need to forgive?" The list was always far longer than I'd imagined.

So don't rush this step. The staggering promise of the Holy Spirit is that he will lead you into all truth, including this one. When you're ready to make this list, you can use initials if you're worried about a paper trail, but do it in a place with no distractions, and when you aren't hemmed in by time. Let God lead you through the process.

2. *Quantify the debt.* Here's the hard part. Dig down deep and figure out exactly what it is they owe you. This may take a bit of emotional energy. What is it they've taken from you? The goal of this step is to quantify the debt. It's impossible to forgive someone if you don't know what you're forgiving them for.

This is why you cannot minimize the offense. In the aftermath of what they said or did, what did it rob you of? Did they steal your position at work, or respect from your peers? Did they take money from you? How much? Did they rob you of your self-esteem, or your friend, or your promotion?

What is it they owe you? What have they cost you? Be as specific as possible, and write it down. Then...

3. *Destroy it.* Go make a fire in your backyard or your fireplace. Take that piece of paper, and burn it. Reduce it to ashes. Make sure that none of that ink remains, and that the chemical bonds that held the words together are dissolved.

This is a symbol of the choice you've made—you have canceled their debt. You've let go, and you'll let God take over. You're giving up the right to forcefully take back that which was taken from you. By burning this sheet of paper, you're giving up your right to revenge.

In my experience—and that of countless others I know—this process is unbelievably freeing. It's emotional on a level that some people have never felt before. The release that happens in a moment like this reverberates on a cosmic level, because for some it's the unchaining and jailbreaking experience they've been waiting on for years. After all, "It is for freedom Christ has set us free!" (Galatians 5:1).

Here's my invitation to you. Take some time. Pray about it. Ask the Lord where unforgiveness might be hiding in your heart. The Spirit will lead you. Write down any names he brings up, and go through this process. Don't short-circuit it, or rush it. Ask God to reveal who you need to forgive.

It doesn't matter how strong you are; you cannot hold on to the hurt without it hurting you. To believe otherwise is to embrace a lie through and through.

The change that comes from a choice like this is no less than life-altering. Something amazing happens when you break the power of darkness in a stronghold like this.

After you make the choice to forgive, the feelings will follow. They'll follow your willful act and faithful heart. It may come a little at a time, over a long period, but it *will* come. The miraculous thing about forgiveness is that if you make the choice to forgive, *eventually your feelings will follow.*

If you make a decision like this, eventually one day you'll wake up and not think about that moment or that event. You'll go a day, then a week, then a month without seeing that person's face in your thoughts. When forgiveness works its way through your heart, soul, and redemptive memory, you won't freeze when someone mentions their name, or overreact when you're reminded of it. You'll be free—gloriously free! The way God meant for you to be.

This may be simple, but it's anything but easy. Some of these wounds don't resolve quickly or easily. If you've been the victim of abuse or a lifetime of mistreatment, the timeline of this process won't look linear or clean. My mother was the victim of abuse that spanned the majority of her childhood, and it took her more than a decade of counseling to even comprehend. I can remember her working through the memories when I was a kid. I would hear the sound of her crying in her room night after night for months at a time. The emotional toll it took on her was immense, and the process took time. But in the end she chose the same path I'm recommending to you—the same path Jesus is offering. It's the path of freedom and forgiveness, even when faced with the gravest of pain.

Forgiveness is a choice, not a feeling. It's a choice we make even when we don't feel like it. If you choose to forgive, eventually your feelings will follow. This has been true in my life every single time.

Don't give the enemy a foothold. He's the one egging you on. You cannot hold on to the hurt without it hurting you. In the end, it's you and those you love most who end up paying the highest price.

13

The Lie of: **Pride**

Life Is All about You

Pride goes before destruction,
and a haughty spirit before a fall.
PROVERBS 16:18

'd just graduated from university, and a friend of mine had offered to drive me home. At this stage in my life, everything I owned could still fit in the bed of a pickup truck, so we hopped in his beat-up half-ton, and after a few directions we were on our way.

All in all, the trip was unremarkable—except for the last few minutes. As we exited the highway and were about to turn down my street, my friend made a decision—one he would later deeply regret. He decided he was going to show off a little. I'm not even sure he could explain where the idea came from, as these sorts of things are more instincts than fully formed thoughts. But as soon as we got on to an empty road, he began revving his engine like we were about to race, then buried the pedal in the floor.

It was odd, for a number of reasons. First, there was no one else there—it was just us and an open road. He was quite literally racing against himself. Second, his truck was nothing special. It was as common as it gets. It was a ten-year-old GMC half-ton, all stock, nothing added. It was like every other truck on the road.

As we were picking up speed I could hear the engine working awfully hard. The V-8 was just thundering under the hood. I turned to him and said, "Are you sure you want to do this?"

He looked at me and said, "I know my truck. It's fine."

And everything was fine, for a minute.

Suddenly, as we turned onto my street, the roar under the hood went from thunder to a whine. Then it morphed into this sputtering and choking sound. If I close my eyes, I can still hear it. It finished with the deafening sound of metal shattering as its final crescendo—almost the way you would imagine it would sound if you put a marble in a blender. And right on cue, instantly the power evaporated, and all went quiet. The truck became lifeless. We literally had just enough momentum to roll into my driveway.

I turned to look at him. He was staring forward, unseeing and expressionless. He couldn't even look back at me.

We had it in the garage the next day. Turns out he blew the head gasket and shattered the main bearing. His engine was toast. We had a moment of silence. If he wanted it properly fixed, it would be six grand, which is a lot of money for a college student. If this wasn't enough, he was supposed to drive back home to Alberta that day—a thousand-mile trek. He ended up staying with me for a week and a half before he could make it home, with nothing to do but think about what had just happened.

What makes a guy do something like that? (Wives have been asking that question for as long as there have been marriages.) Why didn't my friend quit while he was ahead? I all but begged him to stop. But he ignored every escape I gave him, and in the process blew up his engine.

What makes a person so susceptible to bad ideas, and so immune to wise advice?

One word. We all know what it is.

Pride.

We often don't realize it until it's far too late, but the root of so much of the trouble we find ourselves in is that ugly little five-letter word. In the beauty and happenstance of the English language, the very word is an illustration of its vice—five letters with "i" right in the middle.

If you've ever wondered what in the world possessed you to say that thing you would never have said otherwise, or why you made that choice you never in your right mind would have made, the answer usually has something to do with this curious conductor. Of all the times you were lost and wouldn't ask for directions, or you were in over your head and refused to ask for help—the smug little hand working the levers of your heart was this wildly dangerous thing called pride.

Pride is built on a simple but powerful lie—that life is all about you. Pride is relentlessly self-focused. Your life is a movie, and you're the star; everyone else is just an extra in the background.

To be honest, it's the lie upon which our whole society rests. To our modern ears, *life is all about you* doesn't sound like a lie, because it's plastered on every billboard we see and baked into every commercial on TV. Every day we're brainwashed with its slogans: *You deserve this. You know what's best. At the end of the day, the only person you're responsible to is yourself.*

Of all the lies of the enemy, this is perhaps the hardest to spot. The lie that life is fundamentally about us is almost undetectable in our lives. At least when you're angry, you know you're angry. When you're tempted, you recognize the relentless pull. But when pride takes over, you're the only person in the entire world who doesn't see it.

As dangerous as each of the lies we've discussed in this book are in their own right, none of them quite compare to pride. C. S. Lewis once said that the devil would gladly trade each and every one of them if he could infect our hearts with this. Here it is in his own words:

> Pride can often be used to beat down the simpler vices. Teachers, in fact, often appeal to a boy's Pride, or, as they call it, his self-respect, to make him behave decently: many

a man has overcome cowardice, or lust, or ill-temper, by learning to think that they are beneath his dignity—that is, by Pride. The devil laughs. He is perfectly content to see you becoming chaste and brave and self-controlled provided, all the time, he is setting up in you the Dictatorship of Pride—just as he would be quite content to see your chilblains cured if he was allowed, in return, to give you cancer. For Pride is spiritual cancer: it eats up the very possibility of love, or contentment, or even common sense.[26]

I hate the word *cancer*. It comes with an enormous amount of baggage for many of us. But Lewis is right; it's about the most accurate word we have to describe the effect pride has on our souls. Pride is spiritual cancer hiding in the depths of our hearts.

AFRAID OF HEIGHTS

The book of Proverbs is the metaphoric story of two men; the wise man and the fool. It's an allegory almost, of a life well lived compared with a foolish man's pursuits. Solomon preaches these one line sermons (proverbs) in machine gun fashion, one after another, about what happens to us when we live like the wise man or the fool. When he talks about pride, this is what he says: "Pride goes before destruction, a haughty spirit before a fall" (Proverbs 16:18).

Solomon's warning to his son (whom the whole book is written for) is to be careful when pride worms its way into your heart. It's not just a vice; it's a pathway we start walking down; and it has a destination in the end. That end is destruction.

Ultimately pride is the invitation to think of yourself first. It's the lie that life is fundamentally about you. Pride convinces us that our needs and our time are more important than the people around us. It's the temptation to think you're always right, and everyone else around you simply needs to keep pace. "If everyone were just like me," we think, "the whole world would be a much better place."

The Lie of: **Pride**

This lie comes out in the way we highlight our accomplishments and minimize our mistakes. It seeps out in the way we constantly seek out the praise and accolades of people around us. It's the reason we create false versions of ourselves online and pretend that everything's great, even when our lives are falling apart. I gave up on social media for years after counseling many people whose whole world was crashing down around them, and then hours later reading their status update that said, "Life is amazing! #blessed!" I just couldn't deal with the disparity.

That's what the enemy wants for you and me—to be so focused on ourselves that we don't recognize the danger we're in, or the other people around us. To be so self-sufficient we start to believe we don't need God to rescue and save us, because we can handle it ourselves.

This lie manifests in many different ways. It's a chameleon of sorts. I know in my own life, I feel it lurking below the surface when I can't compliment a friend on a success they've just experienced. I know somewhere deep inside I'm happy for them, and I want them to know it, but for some reason my mouth feels welded shut. I simply can't get out the word *congratulations.*

If you're hoping one day to get married, and you haven't found the right person, it can be physically painful to say, "I'm happy for you" when a friend tells you they're engaged. If there's a tear in your eye, it's not from joy but from pain.

Pride sneaks into our conversations as we name-drop people, places, or things that raise our stock each time we mention them.

In my case, I find myself always needing to get credit for things I've done. I find clever ways to let everyone know, "I did this! This was me!" We had a board meeting once, and someone complimented a response the church had given to a disrespectful comment online. (Maybe you've noticed that sometimes people can be a tad critical on social media.) This board member went on about how professional the response was, and well written, as if it had come from a top-notch marketing agency fluent in PR. As I was getting ready to graciously accept the compliment, it went to someone else. I froze for a moment, trying to figure out what happened.

Intellectually I knew this mistake wasn't a big deal. Truthfully, as a pastor I should have been able to let it roll right off my back. It shouldn't have bothered me in the least. But it did. I was horrified. I spent the rest of the meeting biting my tongue and forcing my teeth together, fearing I was going to yell at the top of my lungs, "*Me!* That was me!"

There's no shortage of examples in the Scriptures. In fact, you might be surprised by how often God addresses this. I made a list once of all the times the topic of pride surfaces on the pages of the Bible, and I showed it to my church. I printed the list out on paper, then taped the pages together. It made a document over twelve feet long. I let it unfurl from my hands as I spoke—it trailed all the way down the stairs and into the aisle. It was wonderfully dramatic.

They were shocked. So was I.

Among all those biblical stories and cautionary tales, one in particular stands out from the rest, at least in my estimation. It was the narrative of King Herod's death, and it's as vivid as a story gets.

> Then Herod went from Judea to Caesarea and stayed there. He had been quarreling with the people of Tyre and Sidon; they now joined together and sought an audience with him. After securing the support of Blastus, a trusted personal servant of the king, they asked for peace, because they depended on the king's country for their food supply.
>
> On the appointed day Herod, wearing his royal robes, sat on his throne and delivered a public address to the

people. They shouted, "This is the voice of a god, not of a man." Immediately, because Herod did not give praise to God, an angel of the Lord struck him down, and he was eaten by worms and died. (Acts 12:19-23)

Galilee was the breadbasket of ancient Israel. It quite literally fed the Israelite nation and its surrounding neighbors. In another round of routine squabbling, the cities of Tyre and Sidon needed grain, but Herod wouldn't give it to them. It was geopolitics as usual. Facing a dwindling food supply, they sweet-talked their way into Herod's inner circle and set up a meeting to kiss his feet, so to speak.

When the time came for the royal meeting, Herod didn't just serve a continental breakfast after setting up a few tables and chairs. He hatched an elaborate self-absorbed plan to wow his guests and impress his neighbors. He put on his royal robes and sat on his throne to deliver a public address, but apparently there was more to it than that.

Josephus, the famous historian, records that Herod wore a special robe that day made entirely of silver.[27]—not the color, but the metal. He planned the timing of this meeting so that the sun had just peeked over the horizon at the very moment he would enter the place, sit on his throne, and begin to speak. In the amphitheater that morning, the fresh morning rays of golden light hit his dazzling silver robe, and he shone like the sun. He was glittering and glowing right there before their eyes.

How's that for an entrance? Herod clearly had a flair for the dramatic. Before the crowd, Herod was radiant—luminescent, in fact. The people could barely look at him as he delivered his grandstanding address mostly about his self-importance. The spectacle was impressive enough, and the people desperate enough to win his favor, that they began shouting, "This isn't the voice of a man—it's the voice of a god!"

Herod's show was going right according to plan, and the

people were eating out of his hand. But those shouts from the crowd were nothing short of blasphemy. As Herod heard them, he said nothing to deflect or discourage their praises. It was his way of agreeing with them.

And although it wasn't unusual for a king to have divine aspirations, this bordered on the truly delusional. Satan must have sat at his right hand and goaded him on—telling him to drink it in: "Finally they're beginning to recognize your true worth! Finally you're getting the credit you deserve!"

Luke (the author of Acts) wastes no time in telling us about God's judgment on the man—swift and terrible:

> Immediately, because Herod did not give praise to God, an angel of the Lord struck him down, and he was eaten by worms and died. (Acts 12:23)

So much for the shimmering god.

Herod's story is a cautionary tale. Pride is an infection that attacks every area of your life. If left unchecked, it's fatal inside and out. As I read this account of Herod, I feel like God has a message for us about how pride affects us. It seems to carry a few particularly dangerous side effects.

PRIDE MAKES FOLLY SEEM LIKE WISDOM

Imagine showing up at work tomorrow morning dressed in a silver-plated robe, then standing on the east side of your office building awaiting the sunrise, and reveling in its rays after gathering your coworkers and giving them a grandiose speech about how great you are. People would assume you'd lost your mind, right?

Yet to Herod, this was as natural as waking up and having breakfast.

And that's the problem. Pride has this way of making ridiculous things seem like good ideas. It makes foolishness seem like wisdom. When you're in pride's grasp, your judgment goes out the window, and you drastically overestimate your strengths while dismissing your weaknesses. When you're in the moment, caught in the throes of its spell, ridiculous things seem like marvelously good ideas.

Muhammed Ali was famous not just for his dominance in the boxing ring, but also for the size of his ego. He was flying once to a fight with his entourage in tow, and the stewardess approached him kindly to ask that he put on his seatbelt. Ali turned to her and said, "Superman don't need no seatbelt."

Without missing a beat she replied, "Superman didn't need no airplane neither."

Be careful. Pride fundamentally distorts reality.

PRIDE PICKS A FIGHT WITH GOD

Here's where the real trouble lies. Pride actually turns God against you. James tells us that pride pits you against the Almighty God of the universe. There's only one God, who sits on a solitary throne, and it's a chair he's unwilling to share.

> Do you think Scripture says without reason that he jealously longs for the spirit he has caused to dwell in us? But he gives us more grace. That is why Scripture says: "God opposes the proud but shows favor to the humble." Submit yourselves, then, to God. Resist the devil, and he will flee from you. Come near to God and he will come near to you. (James 4:5-8)

James has never been accused of pulling punches, and this is no exception. When you allow pride to rule inside your heart, you turn the hand of God from working for you to working against you. Life becomes infinitely more difficult. You know how hard life can be all on its own. Imagine how much harder it can be when God is actively resisting you!

"God opposes the proud." He joins the other team, no matter what team you're facing. In those moments, you actually decrease your help and increase the forces opposing you. No exchange could be more foolish.

And no sooner does James mention pride in this passage than he talks about the devil—the two are inextricably linked.

Pride is declaring war on the God of the universe, and James tells us that submission to God is the only treaty that can fix it.

The foolishness of pride is that it ultimately ignores God, whether we do it consciously or not. Listen to C. S. Lewis again:

> A proud man is always looking down on things and people, and, of course, as long as you're looking down, you cannot see what is above you.[28]

PRIDE DRIVES EVERYONE ELSE AWAY

This one is easily the most visible. Think of how you feel when a friend of yours suffers from a swollen head—especially when it's grown so large that it barely fits through the door. Think of how you feel when your friend goes on and on about himself, or insists on one-upping your every story as soon as you tell it. Now, let me ask you: Do you want to spend time with that person when you feel like this? Not in a thousand years.

Rick Warren expresses it this way: "Pride builds walls between people, humility builds bridges."[29]

Pride repels the people around us. It acts as similarly charged magnets. It pushes everyone else away from you because the atmosphere is unbreathable—your ego has consumed all the oxygen.

The ironic thing about pride is that the more it bothers you when you see it in someone else, the more likely you struggle with it yourself. I hate that. I hate even writing it. Because I can't stand it when my friends behave like this, and I know exactly what that means about me.

Pride is at the root of most relational destruction. Go back and dig through the last relationship in your life that died. Do an autopsy. I can nearly guarantee you that pride is somewhere near the wreck, on one side or both. I say this from biblical observation and from far too much personal experience: Pride has cost you more friendships and relationships than any other lie in this book.

THE REMEDY

So how do we fight this kind of infection? What's the cure for a virus like this? How do we disarm this lie that has made a permanent home inside us?

The answer is humility. A healthy serving of humble pie. To realize that life is not about you, but it's first and foremost about the awesome and almighty God who made every one of us, then the people around you that he's called you to serve.

Joy is found when our attentions are in this order: *Jesus, Others, You.*

Humility is a powerful thing, because it does everything for you that pride doesn't.

First, humility reverses the flow in the river of consequence. It restores your judgment. No longer do ridiculous things seem like good ideas. You're able to accurately assess your own strengths and weaknesses and the situation you're in. You can realize that you don't have to show off to your friend who doesn't care how fast your old truck can go in the first place. Your decisions will begin to shine with good sense.

Second, humility withdraws the declaration of war you issued to the God of the universe. No longer are you on opposing sides. In fact, it draws you closer to him than you've ever been. Humility enlists his help.

And finally, it undoes the relational polarization that pride is forever guilty of. Instead of repelling the people around you, humility makes them desire your company. There's nothing more attractive than a truly humble person—comfortable in their own skin, not fighting you for every second of air time.

In my own experience, there's this magnetic confidence that wraps around those who know who they are and who God is, and never get the two mixed up.

I've heard it said that humility is confidence properly placed. It's not inherently self-deprecating or humiliating. What a wonderful definition. Building on C. S Lewis's idea in *Mere Christianity*, Rick Warren said it best: "Humility is not thinking less of yourself, it's thinking of yourself less."[30]

Profoundly simple. You'll be amazed what that does for your relationships, especially in the ones that matter most.

WATCH YOUR I'S

What should you watch for? How do we know when the enemy is worming his way into our lives in this arena? *Watch your I's.* Keep an eye on them. Watch for the number of times you think about yourself, pray for yourself, and look out for yourself.

Let me save you from a world of heartache and a lifetime of bad decisions: Life is not about you. Once you realize that, you just might begin to find all the things you were chasing in the first place.

I often find this fleshed out in my prayer life. God calls us to bring him all our cares, which is a truly wondrous invitation. But sometimes I find my cart is full of nothing else. I spend three-quarters of my prayer time on personal requests, and fit in the other people in my life where I can. Scan your internal monologue and vocabulary for the letter "I"; if you notice it appearing more often than it should, pray about it, and intentionally place your mind and energy somewhere else.

When you identify it, call it out. Pride thrives in the shadows. We need to name it before we can tame it.

There's this beautiful freedom in forgetting about yourself. This doesn't mean neglecting self-care, or failing to do the hard work of introspection when it needs to be done. But it does mean spending not a moment more on it than you have to.

Happiness clearly doesn't come through the channels we think. The great irony of it all is that the less you think about yourself, the happier and more content you'll be.

PART THREE

Your Weapons
Against the Lies

In our battle against the lies of the enemy and against the lies our culture has whispered in our ear, God has not left us defenseless. He has equipped us with everything we need to fight back: "The weapons we fight with are not the weapons of the world. On the contrary, they have divine power to demolish strongholds" (2 Corinthians 10:1). God has given us tools—or weapons, to use Paul's language here—to fight this fight, and if we're going to be victorious in battle, we need to learn how to use them.

We've spent much of this book learning to recognize the lies that bind, regardless of the disguise they arrive in. This process of recognition training will become the alarm that sounds each time the enemy is at work in your life. But there are a few more essential skills we need to live victoriously.

Each of the following chapters deals with a weapon God has given us, a weapon that's effective in every one of the lies we've covered so far—and in the hundreds of others you may face. If you can learn to use them, you'll be well prepared for any deception you come across in your daily life.

14

Discern Light from Darkness

If you've never been conned before, I can tell you, it doesn't feel good.

I was in Washington D.C. on an American history trip when it happened. We took the subway to the National Mall and climbed the stairs to the open courtyard. We'd spent so long underground, we felt like subterranean cave-dwellers surfacing for the very first time. When our eyes adjusted to the light, it was quite a sight. The Washington Monument in front of you towering into the sky, the Smithsonian on your left, and the U.S. Capitol building behind you—it was a lot to take in.

Thankfully when we emerged from beneath the earth, there was a guide who met us ready to help. He was thoughtful, kind, and knowledgeable about the area. He showed us some identification, handed us all tourist guides to D.C., and started explaining the map. One by one he pointed out each of the places and highlighted the history that was written in or commemorated by each. His presentation was second to none.

After giving us the lay of the land, he explained why he was here. Washington has one of the highest rates of homelessness in the U.S.—actually the highest—and they were in desperate need of a new shelter. The plans had been drawn, and the ground had been broken, but they were $400,000 short of completion.

Volunteers like himself were offering these orientations to raise the rest. Would we be willing to contribute?

How could we not? What kind of monster would say no to a question like that? Here we were touring the continent for fun while some people didn't even have a roof over their heads. Between the five of us, we emptied our wallets and toured on. But as soon as he walked away, I couldn't shake the feeling that something was wrong. Actually, I was the only one of our group who discreetly withheld from the fund. It wasn't just because my wallet creaks when it opens, though that isn't far from the truth. I couldn't put my finger on it, but something wasn't right.

Five minutes later, as my friends raked me over the coals for being a heartless grinch, we walked past a magazine rack full of brochures. Actually, they were the exact brochures our guide handed us. They were sitting there, oddly enough, free for the taking. Then we thought back to the ID he'd shown us, and realized it was just his out-of-state driver's license. He talked so fast in an unbroken stream, we'd hardly noticed at the time. And as we stood there, the realization sank in. It felt like a three-hundred-pound weight.

There was no homeless shelter.

Not a dime of that money was going to charity.

He must have seen us coming a mile away.

That story still haunts me. Not just for the fact that we were taken advantage of, but that there are people out there who would say literally anything to make a buck. I'll never forget what that felt like in the moment. It's seared into my memory. As we listened to him talk, I couldn't explain to you why I didn't trust him, but I knew somewhere deep inside that I shouldn't.

Have you ever felt that?

I couldn't give you any reasons, nor could I point to any flaws. I just had a sense that was instinctual. Visceral. Spiritual even.

That feeling is often the way people describe the biblical gift of discernment. It's a deep hunch, or a soul-level discomfort with someone or the words they're speaking. I've experienced it countless times. It's not always negative; sometimes discernment is an overwhelmingly positive feeling that what this person is saying is from God and should be trusted. Paul lists discernment as one of the gifts of the Spirit in 1 Corinthians 12, but it's not just a spiritual gift that some have and some do not—we're all called to use it in our everyday life. In fact, the world we live in can be a dangerous place without it.

In some ways, this entire book has been an exercise in discernment. It has been teaching us to recognize the lies in our lives that masquerade as truth. If there was ever a time we needed the ability to sift through the noise and discern the voice of God, it's now.

TEST EVERYTHING

The apostle John encourages us to do exactly this in 1 John. He calls us to test the thoughts, words, and actions of the people and situations around us:

> Beloved, do not believe every spirit, but test the spirits to see whether they are from God, for many false prophets have gone out into the world. (1 John 4:1)

By "spirits" here, John means persons—or the words and actions of a person in your life. Specifically John is speaking of false prophets infiltrating the church. But the principle beneath it is a part of a much larger truth: that not everything in our world is as it seems. God continually reminds us that there's often far more going on under the surface than we can see.

Sometimes that negative comment someone made to you wasn't just an accident; sometimes it was the enemy trying to derail the rest of your day. Other times that confrontation with a good friend wasn't just friction, but the Spirit of God trying to get your attention. The practice of discernment is the process through which we dig down beneath the exterior and uncover the source of a given idea, comment, or circumstance. It isn't always comfortable, but you can't live a victorious Christian life without it.

When Peter tried to talk Jesus out of going to the cross, what did Jesus say? "Get behind me, Satan!" (Matthew 16:23). Jesus wasn't confused about who he was talking to. He knew exactly where Peter's spoken thoughts came from. That was discernment.

When you have young kids, Sunday mornings can be stressful. When you're a pastor, Sunday mornings can be overwhelming. When you're a pastor *and* a parent, it's a recipe for disaster. Getting everyone out on time and keeping myself in a state of mind to teach is one of the hardest juggling acts I've ever experienced.

I started to notice a pattern after a few years of preaching—that the one hour before church each week was the time Mel and I were guaranteed to get into some kind of fight. It was like clockwork. Fight club started at eight a.m. sharp. The timing was perfect, and just at the wrong moment I would say the wrong thing, then snap at the kids. The silence on the ride to church would be deafening.

It's funny, isn't it, how walking through the front doors of a church is like a magic portal? You could be all fighting in the car on the way, in total mayhem, but the moment you walk through that door, everyone is picture perfect, smiling at all your friends, without a care in the world? It's miraculous.

If the enemy wanted to distract me before I preached the Word of God, this was just what the doctor ordered. Once God showed me where this was coming from, I began to feel this discernment each morning as it started. One stray word here, one impatient response there, and we were off to the races. But once I realized this was from the enemy—and not just life with my (lovely) wife—I was able to defuse the tension in my heart. Once I knew its source, I could resist it. That's the power of discernment.

You and I need to learn what the voice of God sounds like, and also recognize the voice of the enemy—so that in the moment we can tell them apart.

ASK ME ANYTHING

If there was ever a man who embodied the gift of discernment, it was King Solomon. Sadly, he didn't always follow the wise heart God had given him, but his story is a profound window into this gift. God made King Solomon an astonishing offer. He told Solomon to ask for anything he wanted, and God would give it to him. This was a blank check, with no fine print.

When my kids were young they used to regularly ask me this question once a week: "Dad, if you could ask God for one thing in the world, what would it be?" What would *you* choose? Have you ever thought about it? If God appeared today to you and said the same thing to you, what would you ask for? Be honest.

Money?

Fame?

Power?

Beauty?

A million subscribers?

To be at the top of your field?

When Solomon was faced with this offer, he didn't ask for any of the things we might normally have chosen. Instead, Solomon asked for discernment.

Incredible, isn't it? We often remember his chosen request as wisdom, and it absolutely was, but listen carefully to what he asks for:

Now, Lord my God, you have made your servant king in place of my father David. But I am only a little child and do not know how to carry out my duties. Your servant is here among the people you have chosen, a great people, too numerous to count or number. So give your servant a *discerning heart* to govern your people and to *distinguish between right and wrong.* For who is able to govern this great people of yours? (1 Kings 3:7-9)

When he had the world at his fingertips, Solomon didn't choose position or influence. No, he chose discernment. That's how valuable he knew it was. Discernment is the ability to distinguish between right and wrong, and the spirit of truth from the spirit of deception.

It turned out to be the right choice, because Solomon would definitely need it. His wise and discerning heart was on display next in one of the most memorable moments in Scripture:

Now two prostitutes came to the king and stood before him. One of them said, "Pardon me, my lord. This woman and I live in the same house, and I had a baby while she was there with me. The third day after my child was born, this woman also had a baby. We were alone; there was no one in the house but the two of us.

"During the night this woman's son died because she lay on him. So she got up in the middle of the night and took my son from my side while I your servant was asleep. She put him by her breast and put her dead son by my breast. The next morning, I got up to nurse my son—and he was dead! But when I looked at him closely in the morning light, I saw that it wasn't the son I had borne."

Then the king said, "Bring me a sword." So they brought a sword for the king. He then gave an order: "Cut the living child in two and give half to one and half to the other."

The woman whose son was alive was deeply moved out of love for her son and said to the king, "Please, my lord, give her the living baby! Don't kill him!"

But the other said, "Neither I nor you shall have him. Cut him in two!"

Then the king gave his ruling: "Give the living baby to the first woman. Do not kill him; she is his mother." (1 Kings 3:16-27)

If you want drama, this story has it all. Life and death, love and betrayal. I've read it a hundred times, and it still affects me.

Put yourself in Solomon's position. Feel it for just a moment. You have no eyewitnesses, no forensic evidence, and no DNA testing. You have nothing to go on whatsoever. There was no security camera footage or polygraphs. There wasn't a single sign pointing to the truth about what really happened. It was just one woman's word against another's. And a child's life hung in the balance.

How in the world was he going to make a decision?

So many situations in life feel like this, don't they? When something breaks in our home and I find the evidence on the floor, every conversation with my three children feels like this. As we stand around the broken glass, everyone has a different story, each with an angelic face. How can you possibly tell them apart? I've always wanted to try Solomon's method in real life, and pull out a sword, but the item in question is usually already in pieces.

So what do you do when you have no idea who to trust? What does discernment actually look like in such a moment? The answer was exactly what John is trying to teach us. We put them to the test, just like Solomon did.

Can you imagine the tension that hung in the room after Solomon called for a sword? The silence would have been deafening. The room must have been filled with choked whispers and horrified looks. "He's not actually going to—? Is he?"

What Solomon decided in that moment was to put these women to the test. His goal was to expose their true colors. With a little pressure and a little patience, he pulled the hidden character of each woman from the shadows into the light. His test was a catalyst that revealed the child's mother who would rather her baby live even if it wasn't with her, and the grieving mother who'd lost herself in her pain.

When it comes to discernment, sometimes you need to put a little pressure on it, and see if it holds your weight. Start asking questions. Dig a little deeper. See where it leads.

Have you ever been on a pedestrian suspension bridge? I find them both exhilarating and terrifying at the same time. British Columbia has one of the world's longest. I have this vague memory of walking across it as a child, and for most people the experience is the same. You take one step with half your weight, then once you're sure it's safe you take another. It's almost as if you test each board before you make your way across. It looks a little silly when you're watching other people do it, but when you're the one swinging over the gorge, it doesn't seem so funny after all.

In order to test something, you need to do exactly that—apply a little pressure. You need to be sure it can handle the weight. This is how we test the people and situations around us. We question them, and watch what happens. We observe. We ask God for wisdom. We don't settle for simply taking them at their word. We apply a little prayer and pressure and see what it reveals.

LIAR'S POKER

Earlier I said that deception always has a "tell." There's always a nervous twitch, or some kind of giveaway. There's a glitch in the matrix or a clue that something isn't quite right. So what does a tell look like? What kind of questions do we need to ask in order to reveal what's happening underneath?

Discern Light from Darkness

1. Does It Square with Scripture?

The primary way we test the thoughts, words, and actions of the world around us is by testing it against the truth—holding it up to the gold standard. God will never contradict himself. What he speaks to us today will never be at odds with what he has spoken before in his Word, and this is how we identify the counterfeit. Your first step is always to compare it with the truth in Scripture.

The Bible doesn't have a chapter and verse for every single situation you'll ever encounter. If it did, it would be a million pages long, and even then it wouldn't be exhaustive enough. But there are principles we can learn that apply to each and every challenge we face. Our job is (a) to take in as much of his Word as we can, (b) to sharpen our discernment, and (c) to go digging for the answer when we aren't sure.

Many Christians struggle with reading their Bibles. Often they're intimidated by its size or by their own lack of experience. But the Bible doesn't have to be a scary book. The more you read it, the more it will come alive. In *Eat This Book,* Eugene Peterson wrote extensively on a practice that Christians have been using for centuries called Lectio Divina. Truth be told, I bought his book for the title alone, but it became a rich source of wisdom in my life. Lectio Divina is a simple yet profound way for everyone to read the Bible. It has six steps to use as a guide when you read:

Stop (silencio): Pause for a moment to still your mind and heart. Don't rush into your reading. Often we read while still thinking about the last thing on our minds.

Read (lectio): Read it once through and make a few notes. Let the text speak.

Think (meditatio): Think and meditate for a few minutes on what the text has to say, and what it says about you. Let the text read *you.*

Pray (oratio): Talk to God about what you read, and pray it through. Use it as a template. Ask God whatever questions arise from this.

Reflect (contemplatio): Take note of what God reveals to you as you chew on the truth.

Live (incarnatio): Decide to live out these truths in the days to come. Make them a part of you.

If you want an even simpler version of this method, you can try *Read, Chew, Pray, Do*—my condensed version of Lectio Divina. If you begin to read the Word of God this way, it will strengthen your discernment. It will remind you—each time you're at a crossroads—of truths God has already revealed to you.

When your thoughts or the words of someone else don't match with what God has already said, you can be sure it's not from him.

2. Does the Tree Match Its Fruit?

The second way we can test the things we're hearing is by watching the effect these thoughts and ideas are having in the lives of the people saying them, or in your own heart. Jesus said: "By their fruit you will recognize them. Do people pick grapes from thornbushes, or figs from thistles? Likewise, every good tree bears good fruit, but a bad tree bears bad fruit" (Matthew 7:16-17).

If you're wondering about a person who's saying something new and different, watch their lives—watch their fruit. Give it some time. See if what they say matches who they are. Ask yourself: Is it producing a life that looks more and more like Jesus? Watch what they're like behind closed doors. That's often far more telling than the stage. What are they like when they think no one's watching? I'm heartbroken by all the celebrity pastors who have fallen during the last few years. Every month I read about another one, and it's a cold reminder of this truth. Not everything is as it seems.

Paul gives us a sieve to run everything through: Is it producing *love, joy, peace, patience, kindness, goodness, gentleness, faithfulness,* and *self-control*? These are the fruit of the Spirit listed by Paul (in Galatians 5:22-23). Is this what your thoughts are creating in you? If not, there's a tell.

Good trees bear good fruit. Bad trees will produce the only thing they can—bad fruit. This is how Solomon caught the impostor; this is how he knew which woman was not the child's mother, and that she was lying.

Solomon knew what love looks like, and this wasn't it.

You and I need to become practiced at doing the same.

3. Do Wise Followers of Jesus Agree?

We often think of community as a way to meet our needs for relationship and enjoy the tremendous benefits of human connection, but it's also a powerful tool in our arsenal for detecting lies. Whenever you're faced with an idea, thought, or individual you aren't sure what to make of, bring it to wise followers of Jesus. Discernment is rarely a solitary task. Talk with people you deeply respect about the questions you have, and draw on the accumulated wisdom of many lifetimes, not just your own.

Those around you have an added advantage in the quest to unearth the lies you've believed; they have *perspective*. Their vantage point is higher in some ways than your own. They can see your life and hear your words without the blind spots that we all carry. Every single one of us has people and truths that we're blind to. For whatever reason, we simply cannot see them for what they are. This is why community is so essential. The people around you are invaluable help in detecting the lies buried so deeply inside you that you haven't even thought to question them.

Live your life surrounded by people you trust and respect, people who are further along this journey of faith. Find a few mentors, then bring them in on the questions you cannot answer and the situations that are unclear.

Remember, discernment multiplies in community.

ASK FOR IT

Solomon needed discernment, so he asked for it—and that's exactly where we need to start. Ask God to reveal to you what's going on beneath the surface. Refuse to take things at face value. Test the thoughts and situations you're facing. If you want to grow in wisdom, ask God for it! James tells us it's a prayer God always answers: "If any of you lacks wisdom, you should ask God, who gives generously to all without finding fault, and it will be given to you" (James 1:5).

If we're going to live a victorious life in Christ, we must learn to discern. There are simply too many lies floating around.

Discernment is a skill that you'll grow in for the rest of your life, but it begins with a simple prayer. It was the same for Solomon. He began with this prayer to the Lord: "Give your servant a discerning heart." That's a fabulous place to start. Start each day this week with that prayer, and see how God reveals himself to you!

15

Pray for Power

A little over ten years ago, for our fifth wedding anniversary, my wife and I traveled down to Indianapolis to watch a Colts football game—we were big Peyton Manning fans, and loved to watch him play. We decided to make a weekend of it, taking in the city while we were there.

We drove down, had a blast, and were about to park near Lucas Oil Stadium when disaster struck. Somewhere downtown we'd driven over a nail, and it stranded us with a flat.

It was actually quite a big deal. We were two hours from kickoff, and four hundred miles from home. We were supposed to drive back that very night to our eighteen-month-old son. In a couple of hours, all the repair shops would be closing down for the day. In fact, since it was game day in a football town, most of them had closed already.

I'd never changed a tire before, so I dug in the back, hauled out the jack, and lifted up the van. When I'd jacked it up as far as it could go, I realized I'd put the jack in the wrong spot—the tire still wasn't off the ground, though the jack was fully extended. I tried to get it back down, but it wouldn't move. So the drama wasn't over; actually, it was just beginning.

As I tried to loosen the bolts, my hand kept slipping and dragging on the pavement. It wasn't pretty. I shredded the skin across my knuckles, and I was bleeding all over the place. (Those who know me are surprised by none of this.) As I kept trying to remove the tire, it wouldn't budge, and I knew I was in trouble.

So I did what I should always do in situations like this. I began to pray. It was a simple prayer. One I pray often.

"Lord, *help!*"

Again and again I prayed the same prayer I'd been praying since I was a kid. Only this time, the worse it got, I knew I needed to be more specific. I knew I needed more than an extra set of hands. I needed a mechanic. So I prayed, "Lord, send me a mechanic!" James did say that sometimes we do not have because we fail to ask.

Game time was getting close, and hundreds of people were streaming by my little disaster zone. As each of them passed, I prayed, "Lord, send me a mechanic." Hundreds of people passed by without a glance or an offer of help. Nobody stopped. Not a soul. No one even made eye contact. By then I knew I had to get a little bolder.

I stood beside the van, on the sidewalk, looking as pathetic as I possibly could. I made sure my bloody hand was clearly visible, and put a clueless look on my face—which wasn't hard to produce. Still, no one would stop. It was like the parable of the good Samaritan translated two thousand years into the future. I think some people even crossed over to the other side of the street to avoid us.

As I prayed again, "Lord send me a mechanic," I decided to simply ask someone for help. I was out of options. A minute later I looked one guy in the eyes and said, "Hey, have you ever changed a tire?"

He looked back at me, laughed, and got to work. He lowered the jack, put it in the right spot, and removed the tire. In five minutes, he'd done more than I had in an hour. All without so much as a word. Then he dove under the vehicle and tried to release the spare. It was quite a fight. He even had his son go under with him, kicking and shaking the tire for ten minutes until it let loose.

The whole time, all I heard was him saying, "Have I ever changed a tire?"—then laughing to himself.

Finally he had us road-ready and back in one piece. I couldn't thank him enough. He'd saved us from all sorts of disaster, and I was at a loss to convey how much we appreciated it. I even offered to pay him for his time, but he wouldn't take a dime.

Just before he was about to walk away, I had to ask. It had been bugging me the whole time. I said, "Hey, by the way, what do you do for a living?"

He turned back over his shoulder and said, "I'm a mechanic. Have been for twenty years."

There have been many times in my life when I've wondered what God was doing. There have even been times when my prayers seemed to hit the ceiling and fall back down. Maybe you have those times too. But whenever I wonder if prayer accomplishes anything, I remember that weekend. I remember that man. I remember the time that God not only sent us a good Samaritan, but an expert mechanic at my request. It was one of those bold asks that, once it's answered, there can be no other possible explanation. That mechanic was exactly what we needed, exactly when we needed him—pulled from a sea of humanity streaming by. It was an amazing reminder that God hears us when we pray. Prayer is a powerful thing!

NOT JUST WHO WE ARE, BUT WHOSE

Understanding the lies of the enemy is incredibly important. Knowing how he operates and the lies we've been sold is one of the most underrated and under-taught elements of discipleship. I believe so deeply in this that I set out to write this book. Many of us have been sent out into battle without the faintest idea of what an enemy soldier looks like.

But it isn't simply a matter of information. We need more

than knowledge to be victorious; we need the power of the living God. That's where prayer comes in.

Ultimately our victory isn't tied to *what* we know, but *who* we know, and what he's done for us.

Tony Evans used to say that as Christians, "we don't fight *for* victory, we fight *from* victory!" This isn't just semantics, it's a key truth we need for walking in freedom.

Our power and authority are tied directly to Jesus's sacrificial death in our place, and also to his glorious resurrection. As he took a deep breath once again on that third day, and walked out of that cold stone tomb that had held him prisoner, Jesus won our victory and dealt the enemy a fatal blow.

In the already-but-not-yet of the kingdom of God, our victory over sin and Satan is already won. Past tense. Jesus has already paid it all, and his coronation has already begun. It began at the cross, and will culminate in his return. But the word hasn't reached the ends of the earth. The messengers are still being dispatched. There are still skirmishes left to fight. These are the battles we face every day.

As we fight, we can never forget where our help comes from. We can never forget where our strength lies. Prayer is the conduit for the power of God. It's the means by which we ask him for what we need, and receive it. The enemy fears us not because of *who* we are, but *whose* we are. He fears us not because of our name, but because of the name we bear.

Each day when we wake up, we must ask God for what we need. You simply cannot do this on your own. We must start with a declaration of dependence. We need to ask for strength to battle temptation, discernment to know when the enemy is deceiving us, and an abiding sense of our identity in Christ to fight the accusations he throws at us. We need to ask for faith to form a shield we can hide behind, and unity to stand fast together. Each and every one of the things we need comes from him.

Prayer is how we ask for those things—and receive them.

The way up is the way down.

MISFIRE

The disciples learned the power of prayer one memorable afternoon. They'd been trying to drive a demon out of a boy, but no matter what they attempted, they could not. This was a stubborn exception to a remarkable ministry of authority over troublesome spirits. They'd seen Satan fall like lightning from the sky—why couldn't they cast out this one solitary member of his gang?

Listen to the father of the young boy talk to Jesus:

> Teacher, I brought you my son, who is possessed by a spirit that has robbed him of speech. Whenever it seizes him, it throws him to the ground. He foams at the mouth, gnashes his teeth, and becomes rigid. I asked your disciples to drive out the spirit, but *they could not.* (Mark 9:17-18)

Those last three words must have stung. They must have caused pain in the disciples' ears. Now their master was having to clean up their mess, in front of a crowd no less. Jesus's own disciples had failed to free this young boy. They wanted help, and so did the boy's father—but "they could not…"

This spirit had been torturing the boy all throughout his relatively short life. When a crowd began to gather, and he was thrown to the ground in convulsions, Jesus rebuked the spirit and cast it out.

The amazed disciples waited until everyone had left, then sheepishly asked Jesus, "Why couldn't we drive them out?"

That was the right question. Jesus answered it: "This kind can come out only by prayer" (Mark 9:29).

This passage begs a profound question. It was the exact one the disciples asked. Why could they not drive it out? Why could this one come out only by prayer?

Commentators differ on the answer. They've offered various explanations. Some venture that perhaps there are different types of demons, and a select few respond only to certain types of ministry. We know at the very least that there are different ranks in the angelic realm; why not in the demonic realm as well? This is where many deliverance ministries have begun.

Others think that this was a demonstration of the disciples' lack of faith. The issue was the quantity, and perhaps the quality of their faith. Had they simply trusted more in the inherent power of the name of Jesus, the demon would have run. After all, this wouldn't have been the first time they were rebuked for faithlessness. This is a recurring theme in the Gospels.

I can't categorically rule out either of these explanations, since the passage isn't entirely clear. But I'm inclined to side with a third explanation: that this was perhaps a sign that the disciples had forgotten where their power came from.

In the mess and mania of ministry, they'd neglected time alone with God that gave them their strength. They'd forgotten where their power came from.

There's a remarkable story (I actually find it funny) in Acts 19 about the seven sons of Sceva who ran around casting demons out of people in the name of "Jesus whom Paul preaches." One day they tried this on another demon who refused to leave. Instead this demon responded, "Jesus I know, and Paul I know about, but who are you?" Then he gave them such a beating they ran out naked and bleeding.

The name of Jesus isn't just some magical incantation we use; it's a symbol of our relationship with him and the source of our power. When we forget that, we disconnect from the root of our strength.

This passage highlights and underlines the unmatched power of prayer. It underscores that every battle we fight in the spiritual realm—with the weapons God has given us—still requires one more ingredient: a deep, regular, connected conversation with God.

If you want to find freedom and live the abundant life Jesus promised, you must learn to pray. You cannot achieve those things without it. When I say *learn to pray*, I don't mean there's a style or template that God is conditioned to listen to. I mean only that you must make it a regular part of your life and your daily routine.

Carve out time each day to ask for what you need, and thank him for all he has already given, and you'll be well on your way. Prayer is not complicated. God tells us that a child can do it. In fact, focusing too much on the method of prayer ultimately defeats the purpose. In the single best book on prayer I've ever read, Paul E. Miller says this:

> Oddly enough, many people struggle to learn how to pray because they are focusing on praying, not on God. Making prayer the center is like making conversation the center of a family mealtime. In prayer, focusing on the conversation is like trying to drive while looking at the windshield instead of through it. It freezes us, making us unsure of where to go.[31]

The purpose of prayer is to talk with God, lay open your soul, and ask him for what you need—honestly, openly, without pretense. The same way as a child would ask who needs help from his parents.

If you've never tried prayer, or if you've allowed this part of your relationship with God to fall by the wayside, let me invite you to start. It's the lifeblood of a relationship with God, and the lynchpin of our defense against the lies that bind.

There are times I struggle with praying. Not because I don't love doing it, but because there's always so much I want to accomplish that day that I'm forever tempted to skip ahead. My most productive time is the first few hours of the morning. It's when my thinking is most lucid and fresh; it's also the only time of day I'm not distracted, so I'm able then to pray more effectively. By the time noon rolls around, my brain is already spread out across three different time zones.

You would assume a pastor would never have a problem with this, but inside I'm forever struggling. The most effective method I've found to anchor my prayer life is called First Fifteen. It was a commitment our church took on together one year—a commitment to devote the first fifteen minutes of every day to reading the Word and talking to God.

Of course you can go longer than fifteen minutes, and often that's where it leads. But it's a starting point that did wonders for my church as well as for me. I had people coming to thank me years later for the challenge.

So if you need a place to start, devote the first fifteen minutes of every day to reading about the Lord and talking to him. It will soon become the best fifteen minutes of your day.

Prayer is the conduit for the power of God. We cannot do this on our own. Each morning we need to make a declaration of dependence. There are too many lies out there that are cleverly placed and well camouflaged. We need his power to rest on us, protect us, encourage us, and equip us to live free in a world of slavery.

16

Fight Like Jesus

A few years ago, Tom Cruise came out with a movie called *The Edge of Tomorrow*. It was a futuristic movie about an alien invasion. In some respects it's a run-of-the-mill blockbuster story with a dash of time travel mixed in, but the opening scene stuck with me. Cruise's character wakes up on a troop ship bound for battle. He has no memory of where he is or why he's there.

Apparently they don't use guns in the future, but suit up in mechanical exoskeletons embedded with weapons, and he's completely clueless as to what they're parachuting into, or how to use this suit.

Perhaps you've had a nightmare in which you showed up completely unprepared for something. I used to dream I was in church on Sunday morning in my pajamas, and the ushers hauled me up to preach with no warning and nothing to say. I would wake up in a cold sweat. But *The Edge of Tomorrow* is next level.

The green light flashes, they drop down into ground zero, and Tom Cruise is running around dodging enemy fire and yelling, "How do you use this thing? How do you turn off the safety?" You could feel his desperation.

I knew watching that movie that I never in my life wanted to be in a situation like that—for a thousand reasons, including killer aliens. But watching him in the midst of battle run around with no idea how to use his weapon left a mark on my soul. Can you imagine what that must have felt like? It's an experience I never want to share. Yet, if we're honest, it seems that many of us do, almost every day.

Earlier we touched on the story of Jesus's temptation in the desert. If you've never read it, you must! It's the dramatic story of the Son of God face to face with the devil himself. If I was in charge of those little subheadings in the Bible, I would have called this one "Showdown in the Desert." I've been there, in that desert—not just proverbially caught in the vice of temptation, but physically there, on a trip to Israel a decade ago.

If you were picturing a sand-sculpted desert with palm trees in the distance, throw that image out. There's almost no sand to speak of in that desert. It's harsh, lifeless, and virtually nothing but rock. There are only jagged limestone hills as far as the eye can see. No trees, no shrubs, no streams. It's as inhospitable a place as you can imagine.

If you remember, what's so remarkable about that story is not just how completely and soundly the devil is defeated, but how Jesus responds to each of the temptations that Satan offers. As the enemy tries to tempt him, Jesus responds each time with the same three words: "It is written…" With each temptation to chart a path different from the one God called him to, Jesus replies with a verse from Scripture. Each lie is systematically met with truth.

Jesus models for us a reality we often miss in our battle with the lies in our lives. He teaches us that this fight is not a power encounter, but a truth encounter. It took me years to internalize the implications of that last sentence (that profound phrase was pioneered by Neil Anderson[32]).

If you watch this epic standoff unfold, the one thing that's curiously missing is fireworks. You would assume that if the Son of God encountered Satan himself, the fight would be worthy of a full-length motion picture, or a graphic novel at the very least. There should have been clashes of steel, and crater-forming explosions in every direction—as the purest form of darkness met the unquenchable light.

But there wasn't.

In fact, from afar it was a remarkably subdued affair. There were no explosions, no earthquakes. Just words. Words that determined the fate of humanity. This wasn't a power encounter; it was a truth encounter.

Many of the spiritual warfare gurus will talk about how to bind demons, and their stories will peel the paint off your walls. But Jesus calmly yet powerfully disarmed each temptation with bare truth. There was no need for incantations or holy water, but only for the very words of God.

GOING ON OFFENSE

Paul speaks of the Word of God as our only real offensive weapon. Other than prayer itself, when Paul lists the spiritual armor of God in Ephesians 6, all the items are defensive except one. There's the helmet of salvation, the shield of faith, the breastplate of righteousness, the shoes of peace, and the belt of truth that holds the whole outfit together—if you grew up attending Sunday school each week, you probably colored this picture a dozen times. Each of these pieces of armor is defensive in nature. They're all fundamentally protective by design.

Each of them is intentionally fashioned to defend us from the enemy's attacks and give us strength to stand our ground, which is exactly what Paul exhorts us to do in Ephesians 6. But there's one more weapon he speaks of in this list—the sword of the Spirit. This sword, he explains, is the Word of God. It's not a long-distance weapon. It's exclusively for close combat. This one is designed for when the enemy is near at hand. This is the weapon Jesus used each and every time Satan advanced, and it was how he held him back. It was the only weapon he used to cut apart the lies Satan was proffering.

I'm a visual person. I learn by seeing. If I could have seen what happened that day in the spiritual realm, I think I would have seen Jesus unsheathe his sword three times, cut apart the enemy's deceptions, then clean the blade. That's how I picture it. There was no deviation. He pulled his sword out, made three clean strokes, then housed it back in the scabbard. Each lie was met with the truth of God, and it severed the enemy's power—not unlike removing the head of a snake. In the end, it was the enemy, not Jesus, who tucked tail and ran.

When it comes to battling the lies and temptations in our lives, we need to fight like Jesus. If we're going to be victorious as he was, we need to learn to use the weapon he gave us. Truthfully, many of us don't know the blade from the handle. If we're going to win these battles, we need to get to know his Word far more readily, and begin using it regularly in our daily lives.

One of the most effective ways I've found to counteract the lies that bind in my own life is to latch onto a Scripture passage that deals with the situation I'm facing, and then repeat that passage over and over in the heat of battle. I do this more than anything else. I find a Scripture passage that pushes back against the pressure of the enemy, and I memorize it. Then I repeat it again and again under my breath until it takes hold.

When I'm feeling the unrelenting pressure of fear pressing against me—when I feel the cold constriction in my chest—I say, "God has not given me a spirit of fear, but of power, love, and a sound mind" (1 Timothy 1:7). Then I say it again. And again. I'll say it out loud, and under my breath. Often I'll close my eyes and repeat the truth.

You don't have to stand on a table and shout it. It doesn't need to be a spectacle. Just speak it to yourself, and to the forces of darkness around you. If not on the first pass, within a few minutes I invariably feel stronger. Sometimes it requires a few repetitions until it takes, but it does. The truth seeps into my soul, and I remember why I don't need to be afraid.

When I'm feeling anxious, I repeat these words:

Do not be anxious about anything, but in every situation, by prayer and petition, with thanksgiving, present your requests to God. And the peace of God, which transcends all understanding, will guard your hearts and your minds in Christ Jesus. (Philippians 4:6)

Over and over I'll say it, under my breath. I fight back against the worries and anxious thoughts that flood my mind with the truth of God's word.

If you find it difficult to memorize Scripture, write out the verse on a business card and stick it in your wallet. Make it readily available. Put it on the wallpaper of your phone.

I find that faithless thoughts are so often driven from my mind when I'm willing to meet them with the truth.

So learn to use your sword. When a verse speaks to you, find a way to get it inside you.

Spend time learning and meditating on other Scriptures throughout the Bible. The enemy doesn't make appointments in advance! Memorizing Scripture has gone out of style in much of Christendom, thanks to the world being at your fingertips, but you never know when you're going to need them. Just ask Jesus.

A LIFE OF CRIME

When my kids were really young, one of my favorite things about them was their inability to lie. None of them were any good at it. (Thank you, Lord.) Whenever they were up to something, you could always see it written all over their faces. More than once one of them yelled from upstairs out of the blue, "Hey, Mom and Dad, don't come up here, okay?" You can bet your life I was up those stairs in a heartbeat.

One day, when one of my daughters was about five, she walked into the house with a mischievous look. It was impossible to miss. I knew she'd done something wrong, but I didn't quite know where to look. Since she had one hand buried deep in her pocket, I decided to start there.

"What's in your pocket?" I asked.

She smiled "Nothing."

"Show me."

Sure enough, five dollars in loose change fell out. As I began to wonder where she might have gotten it, I realized it looked a lot like the emergency parking money I keep in the van. Then I remembered she'd been whining all week about the silly putty that her older brother was playing with but wouldn't share.

Right there it clicked—she stole it! Not exactly grand larceny, I know, but it's a pretty criminal move for a five-year-old. She's a remarkable girl with enormous heart, so this was kind of a big deal. For a moment I was fit to be tied. I was flooded with fears that I needed to stamp this out before it led to a life of crime; if I didn't act now, one day I would be talking to her from behind a sheet of one-way glass during visitation hours. None of those things were even remotely true, but I felt this overwhelming desire to ground her and throw away the key. Before I was about to drop the hammer, God spoke to me. Not audibly, but with Scripture. The words were right there on my tongue:

"Fathers, do not exasperate your children."

The words were lifted off the page of Paul's letter to the Ephesians. *Exasperate* means to punish them so harshly that they throw their hands up. It means to break them. As I kept repeating that verse, I felt the presence of it grow in my heart, and a few minutes later I calmly sent her to her room and we had a good chat about it. God saved me from making a terrible parenting mistake simply by flooding my heart with a truth from his Word.

You probably aren't wired like me, but in general I'm more likely to overreact than underreact, and I needed this truth to ground me in the moment. As it turns out, this wasn't the gateway to a life of crime, or even to being a disrespectful teenager; it was just an ill-advised mistake. And in dealing with it, the truth of Scripture protected me every step of the way. That was just one solitary verse! Think of what you could do if you knew more.

Trust me, the words of God have that kind of power! The enemy, who was watching the whole story play out, must have cursed in the distance. He would have loved nothing more than to drive a wedge between my daughter and me—to start a rift that would grow a little more each day.

You and I are not unarmed. We have a weapon infused with spiritual power that most of us have yet to fully taste. God didn't leave us defenseless in this fight! But you need to learn how to use his sword. You must get familiar with it. This is the final step in our three-step plan of identify, trace, and replace.

You cannot walk into battle without the sword God has given you. So when you fight, fight like Jesus. It's the only path to victory. Memorize the verses that speak to your situation. Spend time regularly in the Word. Write them out on the bathroom mirror and stare at them every morning. Find your areas of weakness and fortify yourself.

Do something.

Because the battle is coming. Right to your front door. And your only option is to fight like Jesus.

17

Walk in Victory

You're probably familiar with the legendary magician and escape artist Harry Houdini. He was a circuit rider, and his routine was a well-oiled machine. Everywhere Houdini stopped, he began with a visit to the local jail. When he arrived in town, the first thing he would do is have the jailer lock him in a cell as if he was a common criminal. This wasn't the main attraction; it was simply a publicity stunt to bring people out in droves the following night. Without fail, in jail after jail, Houdini would escape in a matter of minutes.

This cycle went on in an uninterrupted flow—until one fateful night. The local jailer knew Houdini was coming, so he came prepared with a plan. When the iron door closed and locked him in his cell, the jailer put the key in the lock and turned it backward. Instead of locking it, he unlocked it. No one knew what he'd done. Everyone watched that night as the infamous magician fumbled with the lock, and was unable to escape. Unknowingly Houdini had been locking himself in repeatedly.

Finally, exhausted and embarrassed, Houdini admitted what everyone could plainly see—he could not escape. Only then did the jailer reveal his deceit. The door was never locked in the first place, and Houdini had repeatedly imprisoned himself. "Houdini had believed a lie, and the lie held him captive."[33]

As you've probably come to realize throughout this book, Houdini is not alone. Many of us have been living out a version of that story over and over. Remember, a lie doesn't have to be true to be dangerous; it just has to be believed. And it's these exact lies that have been holding us back and wreaking havoc on our hearts. They're the reason we cannot escape. If we're to break free from the prison cell we've been sleeping in, we must break free from the lies that are holding us there. Freedom is right there on the other side—but we must walk through the open door!

If you've made it this far, then I'm confident I know two things about you. One, you have a sense somewhere deep inside that there's more to the Christian life than many of us have experienced—it's that song playing in the next room that you just can't quite make out the melody. You instinctively know that the freedom Jesus came to bring was meant to flood into every area of our lives, even if you don't have the words for it yet.

And two, you want to experience it, not just learn about it. You want to live in that victory! Knowledge is good, but wisdom is better. Information is good, but transformation is better. Ultimately Jesus meant for us to experience this victory in the everyday battles of our lives. Jesus promised us an abundant life, and we should settle for nothing less!

The challenge now is to remain alert and refuse to fall back asleep—to take what you've learned and apply it. To keep your ears open, constantly scanning the situations you face and the thoughts in your head for the patterns you now know. To put your recognition training to good use. Then as soon as you identify the lies, trace them back to their source, and replace them.

The blessing comes not from the hearing, Jesus said, but from the doing. And you'll notice each time you practice this, you'll walk in more and more freedom and victory.

This has been a basic training of sorts, but the real battles lie ahead. They begin tomorrow morning as your feet hit the floor. But you're now armed and trained, knowing that you have the living God by your side and his truth in your heart. May you come to know the life-changing power of his presence and truth—and walk in victory!

> *"And you will know the truth,*
> *and the truth will set you free."*
> JOHN 8:32

Notes

1 Charles Spurgeon, (commonly attested, but source material not officially documented)

2 John Mark Comer, *Live No Lies* (Colorado Springs: Waterbrook, 2021), 50.

3 Craig Groeschel, *Winning the War in Your Mind: Change Your Thinking, Change Your Life* (Grand Rapids, Michigan: Zondervan, 2021), 102.

4 https://www.verywellmind.com/what-is-a-cognitive-bias.

5 Based on the quote "The great enemy of communication, we find, is the illusion of it," in William Hollingsworth Whyte, "Is Anybody Listening?" *Fortune* magazine (September 1950), 174.

6 Often attributed to Augustine, this saying actually evolved from a statement written by the seventeenth-century German theologian Rupertus Meldenius. See Mark Ross, "In Essentials, Unity…" article at Ligonier.org, September 1, 2009; https://www.ligonier.org/learn/articles/essentials-unity-non-essentials-liberty-all-things.

7 G. K. Chesterton, *The Thing: Why I Am a Catholic* (London: Sheed & Ward, 1929), 35.

8 Robert Leahy, *The Worry Cure: Seven Steps to Stop Worry from Stopping You* (New York: Harmony Books, 2005), 18.

9 https://blog.ficm.org/blog/freedom-from-fear.

10 Daniel Kahneman, *Thinking Fast and Slow* (New York: Farrar, Straus and Giroux, 2011.), 43.

11 From notes I took years ago at a weekend conference.

12 https://www.huffpost.com/entry/san-francisco-train-shooting_n_4066930.

13 John Mark Comer, *The Ruthless Elimination of Hurry*, (United States: Crown Publishing, 2021), 54.

14 https://www.bbc.com/news/technology-59952557.

15 https://abcnews.go.com/US/teens-spend-hours-screens-entertainment-day-report/story?id=66607555.

16 https://manifold.umn.edu/read/the-perversity-of-things-hugo-gernsback-on-media-tinkering-and-scientifiction/section/69697807-3c5f-4de5-aa3b-d070728205f9

17 https://www.bbc.com/future/article/20170526-inside-the-quietest-place-on-earth

18 Adapted from Craig Groeschel, *Winning the War in Your Mind: Change Your Thinking, Change Your Life* (Grand Rapids, Michigan: Zondervan, 2021), 182.

19 The Greek word translated as rejoice is *charis,* which also translates many times in the New Testament as grace. It has a few definitions, one of which being 'lean towards.' When we choose to rejoice, we are choosing to lean towards the grace of God in the situation we are in, instead of the emotions of pain and frustration we might be tempted to experience.

20 Craig Groeschel, *Winning the War in Your Mind: Change Your Thinking, Change Your Life* (Grand Rapids, Michigan: Zondervan, 2021), 183.

21 C. S. Lewis. *The Weight of Glory* (New York: Macmillan, 1949), 26.

22 A. W. Tozer, *The Knowledge of the Holy* (Harrisburg, Pennsylvania:: Christian Publications, 1961), 1.

23 Anne Lamott, *Travelling Mercies: Some Thoughts on Faith.* (New York: Knopf Doubleday, 2000), 120.

24 N. T. Wright,. *Matthew for Everyone: Part Two* (Louisville: Westminster John Knox Press, 2004), 40.

25 N. T. Wright,. *Matthew for Everyone: Part Two* (Louisville: Westminster John Knox Press, 2004), 39.

26 C. S. Lewis, *Mere Christianity*, (New York: Harper Collins, 1952) 125.

27 Josephus, *Antiquities of the Jews*, XIX, chapter 8, section 2.

28 C. S. Lewis, *Mere Christianity*. (New York: Macmillan, 1952), 124.

29 Rick Warren, *The Purpose-Driven Life: What on Earth Am I Here for?* (Grand Rapids, Michigan: Zondervan, 2002), 148.

30 Rick Warren, *The Purpose-Driven Life: What on Earth Am I Here for?* (Grand Rapids, Michigan: Zondervan, 2002), 134.

31 Paul E. Miller, *A Praying Life: Connecting with God in a Distracting World* (Colorado Springs: NavPress, 2017), 8.

32 Neil T. Anderson and Joanne Anderson, *Daily in Christ* (Eugene, Oregon: Harvest House Publishers, 2000), 21.

33 Craig Groeschel, *Winning the War in Your Mind: Change Your Thinking, Change Your Life* (Grand Rapids, Michigan: Zondervan, 2021), 18.

Go to www.chrisquiring.com
for free discussion questions
and to sign up for Chris' monthly newsletter.